Scottish Life
1500–1750

Sydney Wood

Stanley Thornes (Publishers) Ltd

CONTENTS

INTRODUCTION

Claypotts Castle

Look carefully at these two houses. Both of them were once family homes. Both were built for people who had more money than most ordinary people. Both were built during the years 1500–1750, the period covered by this book. But notice how different they are. **A** is Claypotts Castle. It was built near the beginning of the period. **B** is the House of Dun. It was built near the end of the period. What does the fact that they are so different tell you about how life changed in Scotland during these years?

This is a History book. The words and pictures in it will help your understanding of the past in a number of ways.

- You will develop an understanding of people's lives and of events that happened. Some of these events have been very important indeed in helping to make Scotland the kind of country it is today.

- As these pictures show, there are some things that don't change. We all need homes, for example. But the kind of homes we live in do change. There are reasons for these changes too.

- The people and events described in this book need to be sorted out in terms of time. If they aren't arranged in the right order, it will be very difficult to understand what happened.

- The two buildings were built by people in the past. They provide us with evidence of what life was like. You will find other sorts of evidence in this book.

- Should we keep these buildings? Are they so important that nothing must be allowed to harm them? Is it right to alter them? Questions like these encourage us to think about what has been left to us from the past – our heritage.

> 1 List the main differences between the two houses.
> 2 Why do you think they are so different?

B *The House of Dun*

THE PEOPLE OF THE PAST

Claypotts Castle and the House of Dun are large and strongly built. They have lasted until today. But most homes of 400 or 500 years ago have not survived and the people who once lived in them died long ago. So how can we find out about their lives? If the people have gone we need to search for other sorts of evidence, such as things that they used. Think what you can work out now from studying things that people have used. Imagine that the people who live next door often tell you how rich they are, how they eat wonderful meals of fresh food, read difficult books and never have time for television. One day, when they are out, their dustbin blows over and its contents spill out. You go to tidy up and find the items listed in **A**.

What would you think about this family now? If people living 500 years from now were to find this rubbish, what would have survived for them to study? Archaeologists search the rubbish of the past to discover more about people's lives. They dig down below the level of modern streets to reach the past (**B**).

A

- A letter from the bank saying they won't lend any more money to the family
- A 'TV Times' with many quiz shows and soap operas marked
- A copy of a cheap, popular newspaper
- 6 empty baked bean tins, 8 frozen meal packets, 6 empty hamburger cartons and 40 empty lager cans

C *Some pots and bowls*

B *Cross-section of an archaeological dig*

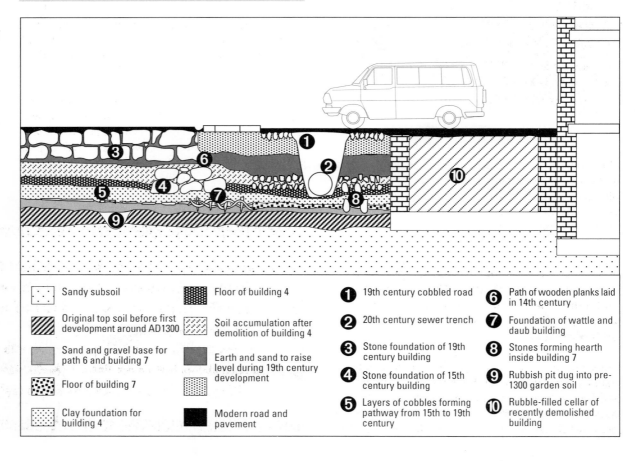

Sandy subsoil	Floor of building 4	**1** 19th century cobbled road	**6** Path of wooden planks laid in 14th century
Original top soil before first development around AD1300	Soil accumulation after demolition of building 4	**2** 20th century sewer trench	**7** Foundation of wattle and daub building
Sand and gravel base for path 6 and building 7	Earth and sand to raise level during 19th century development	**3** Stone foundation of 19th century building	**8** Stones forming hearth inside building 7
Floor of building 7		**4** Stone foundation of 15th century building	**9** Rubbish pit dug into pre-1300 garden soil
Clay foundation for building 4	Modern road and pavement	**5** Layers of cobbles forming pathway from 15th to 19th century	**10** Rubble-filled cellar of recently demolished building

Notice where the period we are exploring is found. In Aberdeen, for example, archaeologists have been digging down and have found many different things. **C**, **D** and **E** show some of these things. What would you be able to tell from these?

 Spindle whorls

- Bones of people, nearly half of whom were under 25 years old. The teeth of adults were far more worn down than modern teeth. The average height of adult males was 1.65 metres (5ft 5in.)
- Animal bones including those of cattle, sheep, pigs and fish
- Wheat, barley and oat seeds
- Fragments of leather belts and shoes
- The remains of holes where wooden posts once stood in rectangular patterns, each pattern about the size of a very small house

However, there are other sources of evidence for us to explore as well as the finds dug up by archaeologists. **F** is a description of Scottish people written well over 300 years ago. What sort of person do you think might have written it?

F If the air wasn't made pure and well-refined because it is so windy, it would be so infected with the stink of Scottish towns and the steam coming from the nasty people that it would be full of disease.

The words used by writers of long ago can be difficult to understand sometimes, but it is clear the writer did not like Scottish towns and the people in them! Was he a wealthy person? Was he a visitor from a richer country? There must be a reason for his point of view

G *An engraving from the 1500s, showing some of the stages in the production of coins by hand*

since it suggests that he found conditions disgusting. Or are you happy just to accept that what he writes is true? In fact the writer was Thomas Kirke, a visitor from Yorkshire. His views may seem harsh, but imagine how you might write about life today in one of the world's poorest and most overcrowded towns. Would you not compare it with your home town? **G** is a further source of evidence.

The invention of the camera lay many years in the future. In the 1600s and 1700s artists drew and painted the people and places that they saw around them.

The sources of evidence **C** to **G** were created at the time we are exploring. They are therefore called *primary sources*. Modern historians who have studied the past provide us with other material to study. Such recent writings are called *secondary sources*.

1 Look at what you are wearing. What would last 500 years to be found by archaeologists in the future? Write out a list and discuss what people might make of all that had survived. Might they find some objects very puzzling?

2 Imagine that you are explaining to someone who has never studied history how we can find out about a time as distant as 400 to 500 years past. What would you say?

A JOURNEY BACK IN TIME

A Jedburgh Abbey

B Slezer drawing of traveller

A number of stories and films today are about someone who can travel backwards or forwards in time. Imagine that you can travel back in time for about 500 years. What would you have seen in Scotland then? The country was so different that it might almost have seemed like a foreign land. You would have seen many large buildings like **A**. This is Jedburgh Abbey. Five hundred years ago, such places would have been full of the sounds of the music and prayers of the monks and nuns who lived in them. All these people, like the rest of the population, were Roman Catholics.

You would have found it very difficult to travel. This picture of a traveller, **B**, was drawn by John Slezer in the 1600s. Travel in 1500 would have been even more difficult.

There were no proper roads. Rough tracks wandered over land that was often wet (because it was not drained). So there were very few wheeled vehicles. Wealthy people rode on horses: *you* will have to walk! The population of Scotland was much smaller then. Today about 5 million people live in Scotland, in 1500 there were about 500 000. If you had travelled up into the Highlands or over to the south-west, you would have found that almost everybody there spoke Gaelic. Most people lived in the countryside, and in fact only about 2 per cent of the whole population lived in places of over 10 000 inhabitants (a small town by modern standards). Even Edinburgh only had about 12 000 people in it. Most folk lived in homes that were in little groups. On the land around them were the patches that they farmed. This farmland did not have walls or hedges around it, though sometimes an earth bank marked the end of farmed ground. The crops grew on top of long mounds of soil that had been piled up to let the water drain off into channels between the mounds. Richer people felt safest if they lived in very strong homes that they could defend, so the landscape was dotted with their towers and castles (**C**).

What of the people? You'd be going back to a time when people could not expect to live until they were elderly. The average life-span was 30 years, with a high rate of death among babies and little children. Girls were able to marry as early as the age of 12 – though most waited until their 20s. What might people have said to you? Most ordinary people were badly educated. But sometimes wealthy visitors came to Scotland. The following voices from the past help us to understand better the state of life in Scotland around 500 years ago, for these are the views of men who visited Scotland during the period we are exploring.

The first is Don Pedro de Ayala, the Spanish ambassador at the Scottish court. This is part of a letter that he wrote in the year 1498:

D The Scots are not hardworking and the people are poor. They spend all their time in wars and when there is no war they fight with one another. They have more meat than they need and plenty of wool and animal skins. It is impossible to describe the great quantity of fish. They have so many wild fruits that they do not know what to do with them. There are great

C Borthwick Castle

flocks of sheep. The corn is good but they do not produce as much as they might. They plough the land only once when it has grass on it. Then they sow the corn and cover it. Nothing more is done till they cut the corn.

The second voice is that of a Scotsman, John Major, who had travelled to England and France too. He wrote this in the year 1521:

E In Scotland the houses of the country people are small for they don't own their land but lease it for four or five years at the pleasure of the lord who owns the soil, therefore they do not dare to build good houses. Among the Scots we find two different languages and two different ways of life. Some are born in the forests and mountains of the north and these we call men of the Highland, but the others men of the Lowland. The Irish tongue [Gaelic] is used among the former, English among the latter. If 2 nobles of equal rank happen to be very near neighbours, quarrels and even shedding of blood are a common thing among them.

The third voice is that of Thomas Morer, an Englishman. He wrote this is 1689, describing homes that had not changed much for 200 years:

F Ordinary homes are low and feeble. The walls are made of a few stones jumbled together without mortar to cement them. On them they put pieces of wood meeting at the top, ridge fashion: it doesn't take much longer to build a house than to pull it down. They cover these houses with turf an inch thick. It's rare to find chimneys, a small hole in the roof carries away the smoke.

The fourth voice is that of a Frenchman, Estienne Perlin. He came to Scotland in 1551.

G The farmland is not very good, on such land nothing grows, there is much bad and wild uncultivated land. The size of Scottish cities and villages is small too. The men are not as well-armed as the French, they have little well-made clean and polished armour, their lances are small and narrow and they have few large horses. Their houses are badly built. There are 12 bishoprics and an archbishopric called St Andrews. There are some seaports. A merchant is highly thought of if he has 400 livres a year and is among the richest men of the country, which is a lot less than the 12 to 15000 livres that is often found in France, Germany, Spain and England. They have barley, plenty of peas and beans. There are many churches that are highly decorated, and plenty of monasteries.

1 Copy this chart into your notebooks. From the evidence in the words of the people of the past, fill in your chart.

What might the people	The evidence for this:
a have worn?	. . . .
b have eaten and drunk?	. . . .
c have lived in?	. . . .
d have thought of the people who wrote these accounts?	. . . .

2 People then did not live long. What reasons for this can you work out from all the evidence here?

WHO RULED SCOTLAND?

Your tour of Scotland of 500 years ago continues. Is it safe to travel about? Are you in great danger? It will be important to know if Scotland is a well-ruled country. You need to speak to an educated man who travels a good deal. A merchant who buys and sells things would be an excellent choice. What might such a person tell you?

A Who is in charge? The King, of course. Who else would it be? Mind you, it's not always as peaceful as this. If our King is not a good ruler or is too young to rule, then there's trouble. The important nobles quarrel and even fight. It was some of these nobles who destroyed our last King, James III. They turned against him, gathered an army and defeated the King's army at Sauchieburn. Poor James. His horse threw him as he left the battlefield. As he lay injured in a cottage, a mysterious stranger came in and stabbed him to death! His son became King James IV, but he was only 15 years old in that terrible year of 1488. For a year or two the nobles still made trouble, some rebelled. Not any more. James is a clever fellow. He'll use force if he has to – like his expedition to the Western Isles to break the power of the MacDonalds. And in the Borders, there is always fighting there. But other nobles he made his friends. The Earl of Argyll has a lot of freedom to manage western Scotland and the Earl of Huntly does much the same in the north-east. The fact is that the King needs such people on his side. He can't be everywhere and the nobles are rich and powerful folk with their own castles. Of course there's Parliament, but it only meets when the King wants it to and that's not often. Certainly not every year! Bishops and rich landowners go there and so do men to represent the burghs. But I suppose the King really relies most on his little group of advisers and officials, his Privy Council.

B James IV

The 'merchant' is an imaginary person. But we can find out more about King James IV (**B**) from someone who actually knew him. In 1498 the Spanish ambassador Don Pedro de Ayala wrote a letter to the King and Queen of Spain (**C**). In it he told them about the ruler of Scotland.

C The King is neither tall nor short, and is handsome. He speaks Latin, French, German, Flemish, Italian and Spanish, and the language of the savages who live in some parts of Scotland. He is well read in the Bible, fears God and observes all the rules of the Church. He is a severe judge, especially of murderers. He is active and works hard. When he is not at war he hunts in the mountains. When I arrived he was keeping a lady with great state in a castle. Afterwards he sent her to her father's house and got her married to someone else. He did the same with another by whom he had a son.

He has revenue from land that is rented out. Another revenue is from duties on imports and exports, chiefly wool, hides and fish. They have much increased. If wealthy people die and leave children under 22 years old, the King is their guardian and receives all their revenues. He enjoys revenue from the bishoprics and the abbeys. Since he became King, the Scots don't dare to quarrel as much, for he enforces the law whether the offender be rich or poor. The island people are very warlike but the King keeps them in order. He went last summer to many of the islands and presided at law courts. The King generally spends his time in castles and abbeys, moving about to administer justice and establish police where it is needed. He goes from house to house, to lords, bishops and abbots where he and his court are given all they need.

Is what Pedro de Ayala wrote true? Consider the following statements about James IV.

He made Scotland wealthier

James encouraged Scottish merchants and craftsmen. He supported shipbuilding, carried out reforms to make coins have a fair value and to make them easier to obtain (**D**). He set up a base for trading in the Netherlands (called a 'staple') so that Scottish merchants could increase their business there.

D *Coins in the reign of James IV*

 *King's College, Aberdeen*

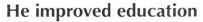 *Falkland Palace*

He improved education

The King was a very well-educated man. He tried to improve his nobles' education by passing a law requiring them to have their sons educated in Law and Latin. He supported Bishop Elphinstone in setting up King's College, Aberdeen. This gave Scotland a third university to add to those in St Andrews and Glasgow. In 1505 the College of Surgeons was founded in Edinburgh to improve medical care. James let the surgeons experiment on the bodies of executed criminals. (He was very interested in medicine and even gave money to servants who let him pull out their teeth.) He allowed Andrew Myllar and Walter Chepman to set up Scotland's first printing press. In James's time Scottish poetry flourished.

He improved court life

James loved colourful clothes and enjoyed life. He liked gambling, hunting and taking part in tournaments. His court became a fashionable place for the wealthy: to better provide for it he began to build Holyrood Palace, and big improvements were made at Linlithgow, Falkland Palace, and Edinburgh and Stirling Castles.

He increased royal income

The royal income almost doubled under James. His vigorous policy of travelling around and enforcing laws brought in money from fines. He even made his 11-year-old illegitimate son Archbishop of St Andrews: this meant that James could draw the revenues of the archbishopric until his son was 27.

A strange tale

James was interested in the ideas of men who said they could obtain gold from other sorts of metal. One of these 'alchemists' was John Damien. James gave him money, and even made him an abbot. In 1507 Damien persuaded the King that he could fly. When Damien tried to fly by jumping off the battlements of Stirling Castle with wings made of feathers tied to his back, he fell and broke his knee. But the reason, he claimed, was that he'd made the mistake of including hen feathers in his wings.

1 Find and list at least two ways in which life changed under James IV.

2 How does the building in F differ from the castle in the previous section? Why might this be?

3 Notice how the government then (that is, the King) obtained money. How is that different from the way our government does this today?

4 From what you have read so far, complete this sentence: 'The ideal Scottish King in 1500 would be good at ......'

5 Is there anything about James IV that might be criticised?

A WARLIKE KING

If you were able to travel back in time to the Scotland of 500 years ago, there is one fact about life then that would soon strike you as very different from today. Scotland was an independent country. James IV ruled Scotland, not Great Britain. Occasional English attempts to conquer Scotland had been successfully fought off and James, just like earlier rulers, was determined to keep his country independent. He was especially eager to increase Scottish seapower, for Scottish traders had to be protected and English warships kept at bay. Some of the money that made it possible for him to do this came from Scotland's ally, France. A French clergyman of the time noted:

A **The Scots have always been the allies of the French King. Without his keep their country would have fallen into English hands.**

In total James provided his country with 38 armed ships, some of them designed by Frenchmen. The most famous of all these vessels was the *Great Michael*. The pride of James's fleet was launched in 1511 from Newhaven where James had developed a royal dockyard, and, at 1000 tonnes and measuring 72 metres in length, it was one of the finest warships of its age. A Scotsman of the time wrote:

B **This ship was so huge and took so much timber that it used up all the oak woods in Fife, except the woodland at Falkland.**

C The *Great Michael*

The *Great Michael* was fitted out to take pieces of all the weaponry of the time. Six long-barrelled cannon poked out through the gunports on each side of her. The masts were fitted with round 'fighting tops' that held men who could fire down on enemies using guns and bows and arrows.

But James's main worry was about possible warfare on land. England was a wealthier country than Scotland and had a bigger population. What was it best for him to do? Should he make a strong alliance with France, since France was England's enemy? Or would it be better to work for friendship with England?

England then was ruled by the first of the Tudors, Henry VII. He was a very careful and cautious king. His main concern was to establish himself safely, for he had won the crown by force. At the Battle of Bosworth his soldiers had defeated the forces of King Richard III and killed Richard. At first James plotted against Henry. He helped Henry's enemy Perkin Warbeck, who claimed that he was really Richard of York, and ought to be King of England. In 1496 James led an army into northern England and attacked several places. But English people showed no interest in Warbeck and, as an English army marched north, James retreated and abandoned Warbeck. Henry VII did not want a costly war with Scotland and encouraged James to change his policy. In 1502 the two countries signed a peace treaty, and in the next year James married Henry's young daughter Margaret.

The wedding demonstrated James's love of show. He had Holyrood Palace finished and furnished. He even had two costly golden gowns made for himself. His marriage clothes included a golden doublet, crimson hose, a crimson and black jacket and a black-and-white cloak. Afterwards the guests dined on wild boar, roast crane, swan, and many other delicacies, before joining in five days of dancing, tournaments, music and other entertainments.

In 1509 Henry VII died and his 18-year-old son became Henry VIII. The new king was a very different sort of person, eager for action, ambitious and less concerned with friendship with Scotland. In 1513 he led an English army abroad to attack France. The French King and Queen appealed to James for help, and the Queen even sent him a turquoise ring and named James as her champion. Despite warnings from his advisers, James could not resist this plea and plunged his country into war. He called on his people for support and 20 000 men poured in from all over the kingdom to gather on the Burghmuir by Edinburgh. They included lords in fine armour on horseback, Highlanders, and Lowland soldiers in their leather jackets and metal helmets. Huge trains of oxen dragged along several cannon. With this force James crossed the border and attacked and captured Norham Castle.

A French visitor, Jean de Beaugué, a little later in the century, noted the problem Scottish kings faced in keeping a large army at war for a long time. He wrote:

D **When at war the Scots are likely to have to live at their own expense, and bring what they need for a few days. During this time they try to meet the enemy and fight in a very determined way – especially against the English whom they hate because they're neighbours and cause jealousy. Once they've eaten all their food they break camp or withdraw gradually.**

Henry VIII had left Thomas Howard, Earl of Surrey, an experienced 70-year-old soldier, to lead his forces still in England. Surrey marched steadily north and confronted the Scottish army at Flodden. James was a very brave man, but the Spanish ambassador expressed his doubts about his skill as a general:

E **He is courageous, more than a king should be. I have seen him do the most dangerous things. I sometimes have clung onto his clothes and managed to keep him back. He does not take the least care of himself. He is not a good captain because he starts fighting before he has given his army proper orders. He says that since his people serve him as he orders, it is not right to send them into war without being in danger first himself.**

The Battle of Flodden took place on 9 September 1513. James had placed his army in a very strong position on top of a hill and he certainly had as many men as Surrey. The Scots gunners proved less skilful than the English, however, in the opening bombardment. Surrey also managed to lure the Scots into coming down the hill. The ground was wet, slippy and soft, so that the Scots army lost its all-important formation. James had armed the bulk of his troops with 5.5 metre pikes. As long as the pikemen remained packed together in great phalanxes it was very difficult for opposing soldiers to attack them. But as the phalanxes splintered, so English soldiers were able to use their bills (or halberds). These were only 2.5 metres long but were strong, short spears fitted with axe heads that were used to hack apart the Scottish pikes. James himself plunged into battle

leaving his successful commanders, Lord Hume and the Earl of Huntly, with no orders as to what to do after their initial triumph. James was hit by arrows and hacked down. His army suffered terrible slaughter. The Bishop of Durham who was with the English army, wrote a few days later:

F **The enemy was far in number above the English army and had marvellous guns and plenty of food. The Scots had the hill, wind and sun with them too. But English bills worked very well. They destroyed the Scots' long spears and though the Scots fought bravely they could not resist the bills that struck them so ferociously.**

Around half the Scots army died, including 11 earls, 15 lords and 3 bishops. James's half-naked dead body was dragged from the battlefield and taken to England.

 Flodden

1 What do you thing is the most important reason why James lost the Battle of Flodden?

2 Look carefully at source F. How can you tell that the author is English?

3 'The French alliance was a great mistake.' Work in pairs, one to argue for this view and one against.

4 Use sources B, C and the rest of the information to work out a talk to visitors whom you are showing round the 'Great Michael'.

A QUEEN OVERSEAS

On 7 August 1548 a ship sailed out of the harbour at Dumbarton, bound for France. The ship's crew had in their care a number of children – five of whom were called 'Mary'. There were Mary Seton, Mary Beaton, Mary Fleming and Mary Livingstone. These little girls were there as maids-in-waiting to another little girl, Mary Stewart, the 5½-year-old Queen of Scotland.

A James V

1 Imagine that you have to explain to Mary Stewart why she was having to leave her home and her weeping mother. Read the following sources to work out what to say.
2 Do you think Mary was the right sort of person to become the ruler of Scotland? By the end of this section you should be able to suggest some reasons for your answer.

Mary's mother, Mary of Guise, was a very tall French noble lady. Her influence helped those who wanted Scotland to continue to be the close ally of France. Henry VIII, however, had other plans. He wished his young son Edward to become engaged to marry the infant Mary. In 1543, the pro-English Earl of Angus and his followers were the most powerful group in Scotland, and a deal was arranged. *deal arranged.* The Treaty of Greenwich was signed, and Edward and Mary were eventually to marry. But the Earl of Angus then lost his control of affairs, and power slipped to Mary of Guise and her pro-French friends such as Cardinal Beaton. The Treaty that had just been signed was turned down by the Scottish Parliament. Mary herself, though only nine months old, was crowned Queen at Stirling Castle.

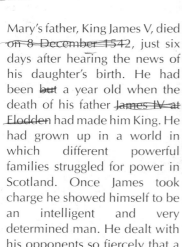

B Mary of Guise

Mary's father, King James V, died on 8 December 1542, just six days after hearing the news of his daughter's birth. He had been but a year old when the death of his father James IV at Flodden had made him King. He had grown up in a world in which different powerful families struggled for power in Scotland. Once James took charge he showed himself to be an intelligent and very determined man. He dealt with his opponents so fiercely that a number of the nobles turned against him, including the Earl of Angus. James suffered from great changes in mood. He sometimes became very depressed and believed that the sad deaths of his two infant sons were due to their being poisoned. He continued the policy of allying Scotland to France, but suspected that his enemies in Scotland were taking money from Henry VIII of England to plot against him. When James led an army south to attack England, he found many Scottish nobles were not keen to support him. The Scottish army was heavily defeated at Solway Moss, James suffered a collapse soon afterwards, and died in Falkland Palace.

Henry VIII was very angry and sent the Earl of Hertford north with an army and stern orders:

C **Put all to fire and the sword. Burn Edinburgh and so destroy it that it will remain a memory of the vengeance of God upon the Scots for their falsehood and disobedience.**

English ships arrived at Leith. English troops stormed ashore and attacked Edinburgh. An English army burned the abbeys at Melrose, Jedburgh and Dryburgh. Henry VIII died in 1547 but this fierce way of trying to win Mary for Edward (who now became King of England) continued: it is not surprising that it became known as 'the Rough Wooing'. The Earl of Hertford now became Protector of England, as

rich families who provide men to king for army.

Scot + Eng Separate

Edward was still a boy; his troops heavily defeated a Scottish army at Pinkie. According to a Frenchman who came to Scotland:

D **English soldiers burned their towns, plundered the low country, took control of all the important places in the Borders, and even had the cheek to gallop about, day and night, up to the gates of Edinburgh, charging about the area.**

With news of yet another English army on its way, the Scottish leaders turned to France for help. The French King, Henry II, sent a fleet of over 100 ships and 7000 soldiers. He agreed to help drive out the English, but he too wished to win Mary for his country. Scottish leaders signed the Treaty of Haddington with France, agreeing that Mary would be engaged to marry the French prince Francis. This meant that eventually Mary would become Queen of France as well as of Scotland. As warfare raged in southern Scotland, the Queen Mother and her friends feared for the safety of the little Queen Mary. It seemed safest to send her to France to meet her future husband.

She was sent to France.

Mary's journey to France was not easy. One of the travellers wrote to Mary's mother:

F **One night when the sea was wonderously wild with the biggest waves I ever saw, to our terror the rudder of our ship was broken. Mary has been less ill upon the sea than any of her company so that she made fun of those that were sick.**

When she arrived in France she charmed the French royal family. One of them wrote:

G **She is very pretty indeed and as intelligent a child as you could see. Her face is rather long, she is graceful and self-assured.**

Francis was a year younger than Mary, and did not enjoy very good health. The two children, however, became great friends. Mary grew up to become a tall, auburn-haired and confident young woman. Her own Roman Catholic faith was strengthened by the deep beliefs of the Catholic French court. She was well educated too. A French writer of the time noted:

H **So graceful was her French that the judgement of the most learned men recognise her command of the language, nor did she neglect Spanish or Italian. She read Latin better**

E *Francis II*

than she spoke it. Her excellency in singing came from a natural ability, the instruments she played were the harp and the harpsichord. She danced admirably. Above all she loved poetry.

In 1558 Mary and Francis were married. The ceremony took place in Notre Dame Cathedral in Paris. Mary wore a beautiful white dress, a diamond necklace and a crown of gold. A year later she was Queen of France, for the King, Henry II, died as a result of an accident at a tournament and Francis succeeded him. There were even those who said that Mary should be Queen of England too. In 1558 Elizabeth succeeded her sister Mary Tudor as Queen of England: Elizabeth was the daughter of Henry VIII and his second wife Anne Boleyn. Many Catholics did not recognise this as a proper marriage, for to manage it Henry had divorced his first wife, going against the Pope to do so. But Mary was not Queen of France for long. On 5 December 1560 Francis died. Mary was deeply distressed. She decided to return to Scotland, an 18-year-old Queen who was now ready to rule her country.

I *Mary at 16*

CHANGING BELIEFS

On 1 August 1561, Mary landed at Leith. Despite damp and foggy weather an enthusiastic crowd cheered her as she travelled to Holyrood Palace. But one man in Scotland at this time did not welcome her. He wrote:

A **Heaven itself showed what her arrival brought – that is sorrow, sadness, darkness and false beliefs – for the mist was so thick and so dark. The sun was not seen to shine for two days before and two days after.**

These were the gloomy words of John Knox, one of the leaders of people whose religious beliefs were very different from Mary's Roman Catholic faith. The Roman Catholic Church had been strongly criticised for some years in many parts of Europe.

B *John Knox*

C *Criticisms of the Church*

- It was too wealthy at a time when many people were poor. It took taxes off people. In Scotland the Church had a bigger income than the Government.

- Many churchmen did not lead lives suited to their positions. People could see that even some of the all-powerful leaders of the Church (the Popes) were more interested in wealth and power than in living holy lives. There were monks who lived very comfortable lives. There were people appointed to powerful positions who were not suitable. James IV's son became Archbishop of St Andrews when he was only 11 years old!

- The Church sold people 'indulgences' that allowed them to be excused from the punishments that had been imposed on them for their sins.

D *Part of the title page of the Geneva Bible in English*

Those who protested that such behaviour was wrong soon became known as 'Protestants'. One of the most important of them was a German monk called Martin Luther. Some powerful leaders agreed with him; others liked the thought of getting their hands on the Church's wealth. This period has come to be known as 'The Reformation', since reforming Christian beliefs and behaviour was so important a question for so many people at this time.

While some Protestants were content to end the Pope's power over the churches in their area and improve the behaviour of the clergy, others wanted far bigger changes. One of the most important of these was John Calvin of Geneva. His followers wanted to end the power of bishops and priests and to change church services from Latin. Calvin believed that only a special group of Christians were chosen by God to escape the endless torment of hell that human beings' wicked behaviour deserved.

Calvinists believed that churches should be very plain buildings, free from statues of saints. They stressed the importance of all worshippers studying the Bible for themselves, and objected very strongly to the Catholic service called 'the mass'. By the time of the Reformation, printing presses were becoming common so that it was possible to produce large numbers of Bibles translated from Latin into the languages spoken by ordinary people.

Protestantism spread to Scotland too. One of its early leaders here was Patrick Hamilton, who had studied at Luther's University of Wittenburg. He preached his beliefs in his homeland: his punishment was to be arrested and condemned as someone spreading beliefs that were totally wrong (a heretic). The punishment for heresy was to be tied to a wooden pole, surrounded by firewood, and burned alive. On the last day of February 1528, that is what happened to Hamilton.

In 1546 another Protestant was killed.

George Wishart studied in St Andrews and in Switzerland, became a teacher in Montrose, and preached the Protestant faith. He found many ready listeners as he travelled about. During his travels he was often protected by a sword-carrying guard, John Knox. Knox had trained as a priest but had been won over by Protestantism. He was a devoted supporter of Wishart. When Wishart was arrested by servants of Cardinal David Beaton, Archbishop of St Andrews, he made sure Knox did not share his fate. Knox later wrote this account of Wishart's death:

E **The hangman said 'Sir, I pray you forgive me for I am not guilty of your death', to whom Wishart answered, 'Come here to me'. He kissed his cheek and said 'Lo: Here is a token that I forgive thee. My heart, do thine office.' Then he was put on the gibbet and hanged and then burned to powder. When the people saw the tormenting of the innocent they could not hold back piteous mourning and complaining of the innocent lamb's slaughter.**

The burning of George Wishart

John Knox preaching in 1559

Powerful supporters of Wishart attacked St Andrews Castle, stabbed Cardinal Beaton to death, and held the Castle for a year until French forces defeated them. Knox was one of those captured by the French. He was punished by being sent in 1547 to serve on a type of French warship called a 'galley'. This sort of vessel was moved along by giant oars pulled by criminals. For 18 months Knox lived on a diet of soup, water and biscuits and was whipped if he did not pull hard enough on the oar to which he was chained. He then spent time in Europe, especially in Geneva and in England (until Edward VI died and the Catholic Mary Tudor became Queen). In 1555 he returned for a while to Scotland.

Knox was a very forceful, fiery preacher. An artist who lived in the 1800s, David Wilkie, imagined one of his sermons (**G**). Knox had powerful friends who were able to protect him from punishment, though for a while he did return to Geneva. The Protestant cause was further aroused by another burning, this time of Walter Myln, a man of 82. A number of reasons help to explain why Knox and his fellow Protestants flourished (**H**).

In 1559 the Queen Mother tried to crush Protestantism. She faced riots by mobs in the cities and the opposition of powerful leaders who had organised themselves into a body called the Lords of the Congregation of Jesus Christ. These men signed an agreement called a covenant, to establish Protestantism. Knox preached that the Pope was wicked, that his supporters were evil and that force against them was necessary. He declared that women like Mary of Guise and Mary Tudor ought not to have power to rule a country, that this was against the will of God. A sermon that he preached in Perth on 11 May 1559 so stirred up his listeners that they spilled out of the church and burned two nearby monasteries and an abbey.

Since the Queen Mother could not crush the Lords of the Congregation by just using Scottish forces, she called for French help. A French force seized Leith. The Lords of the Congregation replied by signing the Treaty of Berwick with Elizabeth I. An English fleet blockaded the French, and an English army attacked Leith. When Mary of Guise died in 1560 the two sides signed the Treaty of Edinburgh. This required both the French and English forces to withdraw, and Mary Stewart's claim to the English throne was abandoned by the French.

Now Protestants were in control of affairs. A meeting of the Scots Parliament decided to abolish the authority of the Pope in Scotland and to end the Latin mass service. It wouldn't – yet – agree to the rest of Knox's ideas, for he demanded an end to priests and bishops, the establishing of a national school system so that all could learn to read the Bible, and kirks which elected both their ministers and groups of elders to help the ministers. It was into this storm of religious argument that the Roman Catholic Queen of Scotland came.

H
- Many Scots, especially in the Lowland areas, found Protestant ideas very attractive, for they could see that there was much wrong with the Catholic Church.
- Some Scots hoped to get control of the Church's wealth. They could see how this had worked in England when Henry VIII was King.
- Many Scots were weary of the important part played in Scotland by Frenchmen brought in by the Queen Mother, Mary of Guise.
- In 1558 Elizabeth I became Queen of England. She was a Protestant and ready to help Scottish Protestants.

1 Look at source E. How can you tell that it was written by a supporter of Wishart?

2 Study source G. What ideas, feelings or point of view do you think the artist is trying to show here?

3 'If the printing press had not been invented there could not have been a Reformation.' Can you think of a reason for agreeing with this idea?

WHO DID IT?

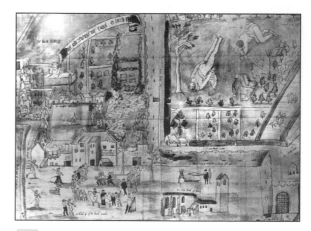

1 On 9 February 1567 a terrible murder took place at a house in Edinburgh. Was the Queen involved? Study all the evidence that follows, then write your report.
   a Describe the events as you think they happened.
   b Who do you think is guilty?
   c Explain your reasons, mentioning the evidence that has persuaded you.
2 Look at D. This shows another murder from this time. It was painted by David Scott in the 1840s, but only after he had found out all he could about what happened. How has he made the scene so terrifying?

He was ready to blame her for almost anything. He wrote:

B **In 1563 there was a great famine in Scotland, but in the North where Mary had travelled before harvest time, the famine was hardest and many died. Thus did God punish the sins of our wicked Queen, the riotous festivity and huge banquets in the palace and in the country provoked God into this action.**

The drawing in **A** was made at the time of the murder. The artist has shown several events of the time of the murder on the same sketch. The two murdered men, wearing only their nightshirts, lie in the top right-hand part of the picture. Near them are a coat, a cloak, a chair and a dagger. But the bodies do not have stab wounds. They are not badly beaten and bruised. How did the men die? Were they smothered? In the centre-left of the picture are the ruined remains of the house where they were staying. It has been blown up, using gunpowder. The artist has also shown one of the men being buried and the other being carried away. This was no ordinary murder. The body that is being carried is the one also shown laid straight out. It was the 19-year-old Henry Stewart, Lord Darnley, the Queen's husband. The other body was his servant, Taylor. How had Mary's second marriage come to end so quickly?

When Mary first returned to Scotland, all seemed to go well. Although she worshipped as a Catholic, she did not try to stop Protestants worshipping in their fashion, and indeed she took as her chief adviser her Protestant half-brother James Stewart, Earl of Moray. John Knox's fierce sermons led Mary to call him to Holyrood Palace. On 4 September 1561 the first of several meetings between the tall Queen and the small sturdy figure of Knox took place. Mary did not try to change Knox's beliefs but complained that he was stirring up people against her. She stated that she was God's appointed ruler and that people ought to obey her. But Knox refused to agree. He declared that people did not have to obey an ungodly monarch.

Mary found many of her Scottish nobles to be dull and gloomy company after the French court. She loved music and dancing. Knox thought that dancing was wicked. She enjoyed parties called 'Masques' in which people dressed in fantastic costumes, or women dressed as men. Her wardrobe included helmets, Egyptian head-dresses and men's clothes. Her main home was a group of four rooms in Holyrood Palace's north tower, but she also travelled about Scotland, going as far as Inverness. She brought several French people with her, including cooks to add French sauces to the many meat dishes of the time.

The question of whom Mary would marry was important to all sorts of people. Protestants and Catholics in Scotland and in nearby countries each hoped she would marry a man who supported their cause. When she decided to marry Lord Darnley, many were angry. Darnley was a good-looking young man who loved fashionable clothes. He was not only a member of the Stewart family to which Mary belonged, he was also

C *Lord Darnley*

(like Mary) a grandchild of Henry VII of England and Mary still had hopes of succeeding to the English crown. Their wedding was a splendid event and news of it was spread through Scotland by the royal messengers-at-arms. They shouted the news from the market crosses that stood in the centre of burghs, blowing loud blasts on the horns they carried. But many Scottish lords disliked Darnley and Darnley was too weak, too unintelligent and too bored by government to do anything about it. The Earl of Moray was furious and tried to lead a rebellion, but too few supported him and he fled to England.

Mary soon found that Darnley did not provide the company and the advice she needed. He preferred to enjoy himself with his friends, wandering Edinburgh's streets and drinking. So, increasingly, she spent time in the company of her secretary, an Italian named David Riccio. Riccio was witty, he loved gossip and was musically gifted. But he was a Catholic, and grew rather arrogant. Darnley became jealous of him and was easily persuaded to help a group of men to murder Riccio.

D *Riccio's murder*

On 9 March 1566, Darnley came up to Mary's room, followed by armed men. The Queen reported:

E We were in our room quietly having supper with a few friends and servants. Lord Ruthven, dressed in a warlike fashion, broke into our room with his followers and on seeing David Riccio declared that he wished to speak with him. Ruthven advanced towards Riccio who had now gone behind my back and the table was knocked over. They then most cruelly took him out of the room and struck him 56 times with daggers and swords.

John Knox welcomed the news. At the time Mary was pregnant with her son James who was born on 19 June 1566, in Edinburgh Castle. She turned increasingly for help to James Hepburn, Earl of Bothwell, who seemed to have the strength that Darnley lacked. Gossip spread about their relationship, and it was widely thought that it was he who had organised Darnley's murder. One foreign ambassador wrote:

F It was made public that the gunpowder had been laid by the Lords Bothwell and Morton who afterwards pretended to be most active in searching out the murderers. They said they were acting for the good of the country and to free the Queen from the misery she had suffered at the hands of Darnley.

Was Mary involved? Shortly before the murder she seemed to be trying to improve her life with Darnley. Darnley was unwell and she was helping to look after him, but left the house for Holyrood a few hours before it was blown up. She left to go to the wedding celebrations of one of her favourite pages. Afterwards she wrote:

G This is a horrible story. Last night at 2 am in the morning the house in which the King was sleeping was, in a flash, blown into the air with such force that the whole house was demolished. Gunpowder must have been responsible, but who is to blame, I have no idea. Whoever it is will be harshly punished as a warning to others.

Yet she made little effort to hunt for the murderers. Bothwell was put on trial but found to be not guilty: at the time of the trial several thousand of his armed followers were around the courthouse. John Knox was horrified by how briefly Mary mourned her husband, observing:

H The Queen should have kept herself 40 days within in token of mourning. Before the twelfth she went out to Lord Seton, Bothwell never parting from her side. Then she went over to the fields to watch games and pastimes. The King's armour, horse and household stuff were given to the murderer.

Three months after the murder, on 15 May 1567, Mary and Bothwell married: the Earl had only been divorced from his first wife for 12 days.

MARY'S DOWNFALL

The Scottish nobles were very jealous of Bothwell's new importance. They gathered a large army and, on 15 June 1567, just a month after Bothwell had married Mary, came face to face with soldiers gathered by the Queen and Bothwell at Carberry Hill. What happened is shown in a drawing made at the time (**A**).

B *Lochleven Castle*

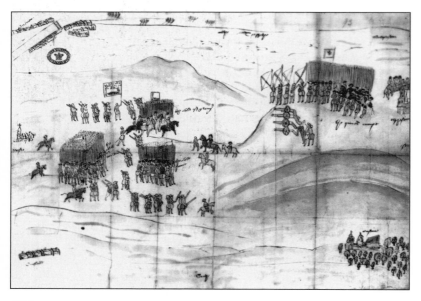

A *Plan of Carberry Hill, 1567*

The two armies faced each other without fighting. The Queen's army is flying a banner with a lion on it and is on the right. But some of the soldiers are starting to leave! By the end of the day the nobles leading the army on the left had persuaded Mary to give up. In the centre of the drawing she is being escorted across to them. Mary believed that if she agreed to give up Bothwell then the nobles would be loyal to her and there need be no fighting. But the Earl of Moray and the Earl of Morton and the rest of their friends meant to imprison the Queen and rule Scotland in the name of baby Prince James. Their army even flew a banner showing the dead body of Lord Darnley with Prince James kneeling by it saying, 'Judge and avenge my cause, O Lord'. Bothwell tried in vain to get others to help him. He had to leave Scotland, was caught by other enemies and spent the rest of his life in prisons in Scandinavia. He died in 1578, insane, having been chained to a pillar half his height so that he could never stand upright. Mary was locked up in Lochleven Castle (**B**).

This castle stood on a tiny island. It belonged to Sir William Douglas, who was related to two of the leaders of Mary's enemies, the Earl of Morton (the head of the Douglas clan) and the Earl of Moray. There, on 24 July 1567, her enemies forced her to sign papers abdicating and making her infant son the new king. Until James had grown up, the Earl of

Moray intended to act as Regent. But even as Mary signed, she declared that she would not be bound by what she was signing.

Mary's position seemed hopeless, yet on 2 May 1568 she managed to escape. She won the sympathy of William Douglas's brother George and an orphan boy, Willie Douglas. They arranged for horses to be ready on the far bank, and for the boats to be chained up so that pursuers could not use them. The Venetian ambassador described how Willie got the all-important key.

C **During supper the gate was locked with a key which lay on the table where the Governor took his meals. The Queen planned that a page, when serving his master, would place a napkin on top of the key and then remove both without anyone noticing. When he had done this he went to the Queen and told her everything was ready.**

Disguised as a servant, Mary was led out of the castle, rowed across the lake, and rode away on a horse that George Douglas had brought. George Douglas served her for many years, and Willie Douglas stayed with her for the rest of her life. Various supporters, especially members of the Hamilton family, joined her. Yet once again she met failure. Her army faced her enemies at Langside and was defeated. Mary had to escape as speedily as possible. She recorded this experience:

D **I have endured 92 miles across the country without stopping to alight and then I have had to sleep upon the ground and drink sour milk and eat oatmeal and have been three nights like the owls.**

She left the country still at war. The Hamiltons and their allies continued to fight, and one of them

E *Elizabeth I*

assassinated the Earl of Moray. The conflict ended in 1573 when Edinburgh Castle, which had been holding out for Mary, surrendered to forces that had English help, including cannon loaned by Elizabeth. Yet it was to Elizabeth that Mary had turned for help. She would not listen to friends who tried to persuade her to go to France.

Mary's hasty departure meant that she never again saw her son James. She hoped for help from Elizabeth, without fully understanding that it suited Elizabeth that Scotland was ruled by nobles who needed English help. Catholics had long thought of Mary as the true Queen of England: in 1570 the Pope emphasised this by declaring that Elizabeth was no longer Queen. In 1580 he announced that any sincere Catholic believer who killed Elizabeth would not have sinned, but would deserve praise. Elizabeth dared not let Mary go free to become the leader of her enemies. Mary lived her life in one prison after another, ending up at Fotheringhay Castle. At least she lived long enough to hear news of the death of one of her main enemies, the Earl of Morton. He lost power to rivals and was tried and found guilty of the murder of Darnley. He was executed in the Edinburgh Grassmarket by a special beheading machine which he himself had introduced to Scotland.

At first Mary's imprisonment was not too severe. The Earl of Shrewsbury was responsible for her and allowed her to go riding and hawking and to have quite a number of servants. If this was not possible, she spent her time in a way described by someone who visited her:

F **I asked her Grace how she passed the time inside. She said that all the day she worked with her needle and that the many colours made the work seem less tedious and she continued long at it till pain made her stop.**

But Catholics who wanted to end Elizabeth's reign began to plot to free Mary. Mary's life became more

confined and she was surrounded by people who worked for one of Elizabeth's chief ministers, Sir Francis Walsingham. An Italian banker Roberto Ridolfi plotted to try to free Mary and bring over Spanish troops. In 1586 Anthony Babington planned to kill Elizabeth and help a foreign invasion. Messages about this were passed to Mary inside a barrel of ale. But Walsingham's spies were everywhere and knew all about what was happening. They used the evidence they gathered to have Mary tried for treason on 15 October 1586 and condemned to death. In vain Mary denied that the court had the right to try a Queen and denied she had anything to do with plotting to kill Elizabeth. For months Elizabeth refused to sign the death warrant, yet in the end did so under relentless pressure to end the plotting.

G *Execution of Mary*

On 8 February 1587, Mary was led out to be executed by being beheaded. Afterwards:

H **One of the executioners espied her little dog which had crept under her clothes and which could not be got out but by force, yet afterward wouldn't leave the body.**

Elizabeth wept at the news, whilst outside her palace, Londoners rejoiced. In Scotland there was little sign of real mourning for Mary. Her body was buried in Peterborough Cathedral, and in 1612 her son James had it moved to Westminster Abbey.

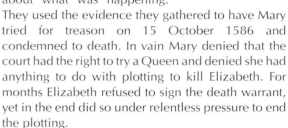

1 Using the material on pages 14-19, make up a time-line of the life of Mary.

2 How do you think George Douglas might have explained the escape plan to Willie Douglas? What kinds of questions might Willie have wanted answers to? Make up an imaginary conversation between the two men.

3 Elizabeth I signed a document condemning Mary to death and giving reasons for the decision. Make up a document that looks as much as possible like this death warrant: don't forget the royal seal and signature.

WHICH IS THE REAL QUEEN?

The pictures of Mary on these two pages were painted at different times, some during her lifetime, some later.

1 By looking just at the pictures, suggest the sequence in time in which they were painted, giving reasons for your answer. Now read the notes. How accurate were you?

2 Which of these paintings do you think a historian would find most valuable? Explain your answer.

3 Which artist do you think felt most sympathy with Mary? How has he tried to make us share his feelings?

4 Many artists have painted pictures of Mary. Why do you think she has attracted so much artistic interest?

5 How might a supporter of Elizabeth I have painted a portrait of Mary?

The paintings

A, B and C were all produced during Mary's lifetime: the artists were people who had probably seen her. A is by Thomas de Leu and was produced at the end of Mary's life. B is by François Clovet and shows Mary at the time of the death of her husband Francis. She is wearing white, the colour that was worn in the French court as a sign of mourning for the loss of a loved one. C was produced by Nicholas Hilliard during the time that Mary was a prisoner of Elizabeth I.

D was produced in 1860 by W. B. Collier Fyfe. It shows Mary being asked to give up the Crown in favour of her infant son James.

E is the work of Sir William Allan and was painted in 1860. It shows Mary taking a last look at France as she sails back to Scotland. The artist suggested that when visitors looked at the picture they should think of the words set down by a French poet who described Mary as saying:

Farewell oh beautiful land of France
You who are so dear to my heart
Farewell forever you cradle of my happy childhood
In losing you, I lose my life.

C

E

F is earlier than E. It was painted in the 1790s and shows a scene that many artists chose to paint – Mary being called to her final execution. Thomas Stothard painted it.

G is the most recent of these portraits. It was painted by John Duncan in 1929. The artist explained that he wanted 'to get at the real Mary and then present her as sympathetically as I could'. His picture shows Mary during the last days of her imprisonment at Fotheringay. He studied portraits of Mary done during her lifetime.

F

D

G

MATTERS OF FAITH

A *Andrew Melville*

Religious belief mattered very much indeed to the people of this time. Queen Mary's sad career was partly due to her being a Roman Catholic. Not only did people like John Knox hate her religion, Elizabeth I supported fellow Protestants in Scotland and they were often Mary's enemies. The English Queen was determined to stay in power, yet during this period the Catholic Church began to fight back against Protestants. The Catholic Spanish King tried to invade England and also to destroy England's allies, the Dutch Protestants. In France, the Catholic rulers carried out a terrible killing of French Protestants in Paris. These troubles went on through the 1600s, especially in Germany, where a dreadful war from 1618 to 1648 caused the death of thousands of both Catholics and Protestants.

John Knox died in 1572. Many Scots were still Catholic but they never found the forceful, vigorous leadership that brought the Protestants such success and eventually led to the setting up of the Church of Scotland. In 1574 a new Protestant leader arrived. Andrew Melville came back to Scotland from Geneva, one of Europe's main centres of Protestantism. He became Principal of Glasgow University and then (in 1580) of St Andrews. He not only spoke and wrote well, he had very strong and clear ideas which in 1578 he persuaded the General Assembly of the Church to accept. His ideas were written down in *The Second Book of Discipline*. Another church minister, who did not agree with Melville's ideas, wrote in 1575:

B **In the Church this year changes began to happen which, to this day, have kept it in continual unquietness. Mr Andrew Melville who was lately from Geneva, a man learned but hot and eager, is labouring to bring into his Church the Presbyterian discipline of Geneva.**

Melville declared that his ideas (**C**) were based on the Word of God as found in the Bible. He believed the Church mattered even more than the power of the King. In 1592 Parliament accepted the main parts of this plan, although Melville did not succeed in winning for the Kirk either all the income that had once gone to the old Church, or the election of ministers by congregations.

- A kirk in every parish — the congregation elected 'elders' and 'deacons' every year to make up the kirk sessions who, with the ministers, were in charge
- Ministers chosen by the kirk session
- Presbyteries and synods — that is, groups of people to oversee the kirk sessions
- General Assemblies made up of ministers and elders, meeting every year, to decide general policies
- No bishops or archbishops with power over the Church

C *Melville's ideas*

The energy and strong beliefs of the Kirk members meant that it was soon strongly established in the burghs. It spread in the countryside too, though it did not become widely established in much of the Highlands. Where it did triumph, it was able to powerfully shape people's lives.

D *A Reformation kirk*

The Kirk expected people to live sober, quiet and hardworking lives. It did not approve of showy clothing – ministers wore grey or dark blue and their wives were expected to avoid wearing rings and bracelets and gowns in bright colours. The statues and stained-glass windows in some cathedrals were smashed – the Kirk preferred simple church buildings that were plainly decorated. The General Assembly passed strong rules attacking the following activities:

E Adultery, unlawful marriage and divorce, excessive drinking, greedy eating, gorgeous and vain clothes, speeches full of swearing.

People who broke rules were punished. On Sundays people were expected to worship, not work, or play games, or visit markets, or go to ale houses. Officially appointed 'searchers' went looking for people who were not in church, to fine them. In 1650, for example, a man in Culross was fined when he admitted that on one Sunday he had been:

F Sitting in his own home the whole time.

Offenders might be made to stand or kneel by the church for many Sundays, wearing sackcloth. Sometimes offenders were whipped, too. Kirk leaders thought that people should remember the birth and death of Jesus all the time, not just on special days as at Christmas and Easter, and so they tried to stop the celebrations then. In Aberdeen, for example, Patrick Spalding wrote in 1641:

G Friday the 25 December, of old called 'Yuleday' and on which preaching and thanksgiving was given to God in remembrance of our blessed Saviour and friends and neighbours made merry and had good cheer: now there is no such preachings or meetings with merryness, but the day is commanded to be kept as a work day, feasting and idleness forbidden.

Anthony Weldon, an English visitor who did not like most Scots, wrote:

H They keep no holy days nor acknowledge any saint but St Andrew. Their Sunday exercise is preaching in the morning and persecuting in the afternoon. They hold their noses if you speak of bear baiting and their ears if you speak of play.

Certainly Scottish people lost the saints' days and feast days, the miracle plays and the masques and other entertainments that had once formed part of their year. It depended on who was in power as to how strict the rules were. Under King James VI they were not as demanding as under those who controlled Scotland from 1638 for the next ten years.

The Kirk brought to people the chance to help run Kirk affairs. It brought the Bible and the services to ordinary people in the language that most could understand – English. Lack of Gaelic speakers hindered the Kirk's spread in the Highlands, nor was there a Bible in Scots: the use of translations from England helped spread the English language. Since the Kirk wanted to see all worshippers reading the Bible, it greatly encouraged the setting-up of schools, tried to provide free education for the poor, and improved the university education which trained its ministers. Melville had plans to provide support for very poor people and to end the need for begging, though the Kirk never got control of all the income that would have made this possible.

Melville's views were not shared by all Kirk members, nor did Scottish monarchs care for some of them. In particular, kings and queens preferred to have bishops helping to rule the Kirk, and for some years this was indeed what happened. They opposed the choosing of ministers simply through election of suitably qualified people by congregations. Instead they kept in place the power of the 'patrons', the landowners to whom the monarch had awarded the right to make church appointments. James VI and his son, Charles I, both believed that they were kings 'by divine right' – they were appointed by God and could therefore not be answerable to the Kirk. Differences between Kings and Kirk played a big part in the events that were to trouble Scotland in the 1600s. Eventually, out of the troubles that are described in the next sections, came an Act of Parliament of 1690 that established the shape of the Church of Scotland for two centuries (**I**).

I Their majesties do confirm the presbyteries' church government and discipline, that is the government of the church by Kirk sessions, presbyteries, provincial synods and general assemblies.

1 What do you think Anthony Weldon was referring to when he wrote 'persecuting' (H)?

2 How might a kirk elder have replied to what he had to say?

3 Imagine you are a kirk elder of this time. You are giving a speech explaining to the kirk session why an offender you have caught should be punished.

TWO COUNTRIES, ONE KING

A *James VI and I*

On 26 March 1603, the King of Scotland had just gone to bed when he heard the excited sounds of the arrival of a traveller, Sir Robert Carey, who came muddy and tired from three days of riding north from London. He was brought to the King's bedside where he knelt, kissed the King's hand, and greeted him as the King of England!

The Scottish King who had become the King of England too was Mary Stewart's son, James VI. Scotland and England remained quite separate and independent countries, but now they shared the same king.

What sort of a person was James? An Englishman of the time, Sir Anthony Weldon, wrote this description:

B He was of medium height, his clothes were large and loose, the doublets quilted to resist stabbing, his eyes large, his beard thin, his tongue too large for his mouth which made him drink as if eating his drink so that it came out on each side of his mouth. His legs were very weak. He drank very often, he would never change his clothes until worn out to rags. He was very witty. He lived in peace, died in peace and left all his kingdoms in a 'peaceable condition'.

Did James really deserve to be described like this? His table manners were messy, he swore a great deal and was very fond of alcohol. Yet consider the kind of life he had to live, and his achievement, and make up your own mind. He was born on 19 June 1566. At the age of 13 months, on 29 July 1567, he was crowned King. The crown was so heavy it could not be placed on the infant's head, but had to be held above it. He was put in the care of one of the great scholars of the age, George Buchanan, who made James study for many hours. He mastered Latin and French, studied history, geography, astronomy and the sciences, and built up a library of over 700 books. He became one of the most well-educated rulers in Europe, and never lost his love of books.

James's tutor was a stern Protestant who strongly disliked James's mother, and encouraged the King to share his feelings. James's father, Lord Darnley, had been murdered and the young King lived a rather lonely life, starved of family love. In later life he tended to show his gratitude to handsome young men who were friendly and who had the confidence he lacked, and showered them with gifts. In 1589 he married a Danish princess, Anne, when he was in his early twenties and she was just 14. The ceremony took place in Norway during winter. James hired four negroes to entertain the company by dancing in the snow (all four caught pneumonia and died). The couple eventually had seven children, though only three lived to become adults.

James grew up in dangerous times. Two of the regents who governed Scotland for him were murdered, and a third was beheaded. Nobles and clan chiefs alike were very ready to settle their quarrels by violence, shooting and stabbing one another and attacking one another's property. One clan chief, Mackenzie of Kintail, was described at the time as:

C A very active man, he burned property and persecuted people in Sleat for his pleasure.

A group of MacDonalds killed their Mackenzie enemies by burning down the church where they were worshipping. James himself was kidnapped for a while and grew up very much at the mercy of fierce men. It was not really until 1585 that he got proper control of the government.

It is not surprising, then, that he lived in fear of attempts to murder him. Sometimes he even piled up furniture against his bedroom door before going to sleep. He was determined to make Scotland a more peaceful and law-abiding nation and to stop the terrible quarrels between the noble families. He advised his son, in 1597:

D Rest not until you root out these barbarous feuds, their barbarous name is unknown to any other nation.

He found that people in the burghs, the owners of land who just wanted to improve their estates, lawyers and many other folk, responded to his policy. He managed to re-organise Parliament in Scotland so that most of its work was done by a group of his friends, called the Lords of the Articles. He controlled the Kirk by bringing back bishops and by sending the highly critical and argumentative Andrew Melville out of Scotland to live in exile. Although he punished one great family – the Ruthvens – who had been his enemies, in general he treated the noble families with

F *View of Edzell from the garden*

Reform and civilise the best among them, rooting out or transporting the barbarous and planting civilised people in their place.

There was some improvement. He used two noble leaders – Argyll and Huntly – to try to control their neighbours. The troublesome MacGregors were hunted down: one Campbell chief offered his men the same reward for the head of a MacGregor as for a wolf! He tried to send peaceful folk from Fife to live in Lewis, but the local people forced them to leave. He made Highland chiefs sign promises of good behaviour and swear that they would learn English and come regularly to Edinburgh. He settled Scots and English Protestants in Ulster to stop one especially warlike clan from getting regular support from relatives in Northern Ireland.

James only ever returned to Scotland once after 1603. It is a sign of how well he had built up the government that it ran so smoothly without him actually being there. A regular flow of letters passed up and down between London and Edinburgh, and James claimed he ruled Scotland even better by the pen than when he was there. He was a tolerant man who tried to persuade people with different beliefs to live together. He tried to be on good terms with foreign lands that were Protestant and those that were Catholic. His hatred of violence and war can be seen in his advice to his son Charles, that, if ever he were forced into battle, he should wear the lightest armour so that he could easily run away. His success can be seen in the homes that wealthy people now began to build. Comfort as well as safety played a part in a castle like Edzell (**F**). And finally, long before the evidence of modern science, James strongly attacked the new habit of smoking tobacco as being very unhealthy.

respect and tried to avoid so offending them as to make them extreme rebels. In any case, hostile nobles no longer had England to escape to and Elizabeth to help them. The Queen of England named James to succeed her and after 1603 James had even more power, as King of both countries. He was able to use this power to make the troublesome Borders into a far more peaceful region.

Families here had long defied the law and lived by raiding, stealing and killing. James held trials, executed many leaders, and made the area more law-abiding. But the Highlands and Western Isles resisted his efforts. James wrote:

E As for the Highlands I believe there are two sorts of people, one on the mainland that are barbarous, yet have some show of civility, the others live in the Isles and are wholly barbarous.

1 James VI did much to change Scotland. What sort of people would have been very pleased? Who might not have been pleased?

2 Scotland had long resisted attempts by English kings to win control of it. Why do you think that now it was so easy to establish one monarchy for both countries?

THE COMING OF THE COVENANT

James VI died in 1625, leaving largely peaceful kingdoms behind him. Yet less than 15 years later, the next Stewart King, Charles I, led an English army to attack Scotland whilst angry Scots organised themselves to fight. What had gone wrong?

What were the causes of the troubles described in this section: Who was to blame? How might two quite different people have explained what happened:
- a strong supporter of King Charles I
- a strong supporter of the Covenant?

A *Charles I*

In 1636 an English visitor to Scotland, Sir William Brereton, wrote about church services on Sundays:

B They assemble between 8 and 9 in the morning and spend time singing psalms and reading chapters in the Old Testament until about 10. Then the preacher comes into the pulpit, he reads a prayer, another psalm is sung, and then he prays before his sermon and ends his sermon between 11 and 12.

The rules of the Church of England are being much pressed and much opposed by many ministers and many of the people.

Sir William had seen one of the main causes of Scottish anger with Charles I. James VI had already tried to alter kirk services and brought back bishops, but when people refused to change their ways he did not try to force them. But Charles was a very different sort of person. He knew little about Scotland since he had left it at the age of 3 and did not return until 1633. His marriage to a French Roman Catholic princess, Henrietta Maria, further strengthened his love of forms of religion in which there was a great deal of ceremony, kneeling before the altar, and services conducted by clergy wearing especially elaborate clothing. Charles was just over 5 feet tall – not only did he not look impressive, but he didn't sound it either. He had a nervous and awkward way of speaking. But he was a very determined man. He believed he was God's representative on earth who ruled 'by divine right' and he was very devoted to his religious beliefs. He declared:

C Princes are not bound to give account of their actions but to God alone.

His reign began badly. He passed a law taking back land that had once belonged to the Roman Catholic Church but which had since been awarded to nobles and other lairds. This caused a lot of anger. In the end most landowners kept the land, but had to pay money every year to the King for the right to keep it. Charles aimed to use the money to support the Church: the way he had done it, however, had given offence. He also taxed landowners on a more regular basis than ever before, partly to meet the cost of wars against Spain and France. When he came to Scotland, eventually, to be crowned, he brought the Archbishop of Canterbury with him and insisted on a service that was far more elaborate than was normal in the Kirk.

He then began to try to compel Scots worshippers to follow services like those in the Church of England. A new book of church rules stated that the communion table should be moved from the centre of the church to the front where it became much more like an altar. A new Prayer Book of 1637 for Scotland tried to change services too. When the Dean of St Giles in Edinburgh, Dr Hanna, tried to first use the Prayer Book, there was uproar (**D**).

Members of the congregation, including many women, shouted out in protest and even began to throw things. The Bishop of Edinburgh had the church cleared, but the service continued with a mob outside shouting, banging on the doors and throwing stones at the windows. Opposition to this Prayer Book was widespread, but the King would not

change his mind. The result was that his opponents began to organise against him. Representatives of nobles, ministers, lairds and the burghs formed a committee of 16. They included the Earl of Rothes (a fat jolly man, yet a cunning one), the minister of Leuchars, Alexander Hamilton, and a leading lawyer, Lord Warriston. Since Charles continued to demand obedience and he ignored all the petitions sent to him, this group drew up a statement of their beliefs.

This 'National Covenant' was signed by many leading people over three days starting on 28 February 1638. It made it clear that those signing it thought Charles was badly advised and that the recent attempts to change ways of worshipping were wrong (and changes needed the agreement of a General Assembly and Parliament) and that the Presbyterian Church was the true church. Charles's representatives in Scotland were too weak to stop it. The King had been ruling Scotland through a little group of his supporters – especially bishops – on the Privy Council. Now he allowed a General Assembly of the Kirk to meet to buy himself time to raise troops, though he insisted it met in the peaceful town of Glasgow, well away from the troubles in Edinburgh. By the time it met, in November 1638, supporters of the Covenant were numerous. Copies of the document had been sent around the Kingdom, ministers preached in support of it and one of the leading nobles, the Duke of Argyll, head of the mighty Campbell clan, came out in favour of it. Charles's representative, the Marquis of Hamilton, tried in vain to stop it in the Assembly. He reported to his master:

E **Truly Sir, my soul was never sadder than to see such a sight, not one gown among the whole company, many swords, but many more daggers.**

The Assembly supported the Covenant, said it would meet every year, condemned the Prayer Book, and denounced bishops. The King now gathered together about 20 000 soldiers and came north to force obedience. But he lacked money to pay his troops and they were not eager to fight. Supporters of the Covenant gathered an army too, flying banners like the one in **F**.

The Covenanters included Highlanders led by the Duke of Argyll. Moreover their commander, Alexander Leslie, and several other officers were experienced soldiers who had been fighting abroad for foreign leaders. The two forces met at Berwick. Charles realised that he could not win and this first 'Bishops' War' of 1639 ended with his giving way and agreeing to another General Assembly of the Kirk and a meeting of the Scottish Parliament. Both these gatherings denounced his policies, demanded the end of bishops, and insisted on meeting regularly in future, so ending Charles's system of ruling through a little group of his friends. In 1640 the second 'Bishops' War' took place as Leslie's army marched south to force Charles to agree to these demands. They easily occupied New-castle and Durham, making the areas they occupied pay for their keep. Charles had too many other troubles to be able to resist. In June 1641 he gave in to all the demands of the Covenanters. He handed out rewards to some of the leaders (Leslie became the Earl of Leven, for example) and he even played golf with some of them! But the victorious Scots were now drawn into an even bigger conflict.

F Banner of the Covenant Army

THE FIRST UNION OF SCOTLAND AND ENGLAND

By 1641 Scotland was free of King Charles's attempts to rule it through his friends and force the Kirk to become more like the Church of England. The supporters of the Covenant, with a strong army to back them, had won. Yet only ten years later this Scottish freedom had vanished and, in March 1652, the English Parliament decided:

A **That an Act should be brought in for incorporating [joining] Scotland into one commonwealth with England.**

The Scottish Parliament was abolished. The General Assembly of the Kirk was not allowed to meet. Instead 30 Scots travelled to London as members of one Parliament for the whole of Scotland, England, Wales and Ireland. What caused such an astonishing change?

King Charles I had tried to rule England in the same way as Scotland. But, by 1640, he was so short of money that he had to allow the English Parliament to meet to pass laws for taxes. This gave Charles's English enemies their chance. They aimed to cut the King's power; many of them also shared the Kirk's dislike of Charles's religious beliefs. By 1642 the two sides were at war. Scottish leaders agreed to support the Parliamentary side for fear that, if Charles won, he would turn on Scotland next. Their English allies needed Scottish military strength and therefore agreed to pay the Scottish army £30 000 a month. They also agreed to change their Church to be much more like the Scottish Presbyterian Church. This agreement was called 'The Solemn League and Covenant'. A meeting of 150 church ministers and others drew up a statement of the beliefs of the Church that was planned for both England and Scotland. Although only eight Scots were present, helping to draw up this 'Westminster Confession', it was the Church of Scotland that was most strongly affected by it. It produced arrangements of psalms that are still sung and a 'catechism' (questions and answers) so that children learned the beliefs of the Presbyterian Church.

In January 1644 a Scottish army marched south. At Marston Moor in Yorkshire, it played a vital part in bringing about the defeat of the Royalists. Parliamentary forces were able to increase and improve: led by Oliver Cromwell they eventually became unbeatable and in 1646 King Charles surrendered to the Scots. The Covenanters handed

B *James Graham, Earl of Montrose*

him to Cromwell, but by now some of them were beginning to weary of the failure of the English Parliamentary side to keep the promises of the Solemn League and Covenant. Those who felt like this held secret talks with the King and agreed to help him in return for his promises to help establish their beliefs in England. But their efforts were in vain – at Preston their army was crushed by Cromwell.

This battle is an example of how Scottish people became increasingly divided by the war with the King. Some had always thought it wrong and had fought in vain for Charles.

Their leader was the Earl of Montrose, James Graham. In March 1644 he became the King's Lieutenant-General in Scotland. For 18 months he led a small army of Irishmen and Highlanders on an amazing campaign, winning a series of battles against the larger Covenanting forces of his great enemy, the Duke of Argyll.

This is how someone at the time described Montrose:

C **He showed the greatest cheerfulness in the most difficult times. If his infantry hesitated to**

D *Duke of Argyll*

wade a river, he was the first to dismount to
show others the way. He accustomed himself to
coarse feeding and a constant drinking of water.
It was wonderful how he kept his army together.
He was pleasant and witty in conversation. In
this way he made war against His Majesty's
enemies, bearing the trophies of six battles with
the defeat of six armies.

Montrose even launched a successful midwinter raid
on the homeland of his enemy Argyll. The Duke
managed to scramble aboard a fishing boat to
escape. But Lowland Scotland did not support
Montrose. On 13 September 1645, he was defeated
by a large and experienced Scottish army under
David Leslie and had to escape abroad.

In England affairs fell into the hands of Cromwell and
the army. In January 1649 King Charles was tried and
executed. This event shocked all groups in Scotland
and the dead King's 18-year-old son was promptly
recognised as King Charles II. Montrose returned
from exile to fight for him, only to be captured. As
he was being led to his death he looked up to see the
Duke of Argyll peering down at him through the
shutters of a window. As an eye-witness noted:

E His sentence was to be hanged upon a
gallows 30 foot high, 3 hours at Edinburgh Cross,
to have his head struck off and placed on the
tollbooth and his arms and legs hung up in other
towns.

Divisions between Scots helped Cromwell to
triumph. He led an army north to crush the Scottish
support for Charles II, winning a battle at Dunbar.
Cromwell himself reported:

F The Enemy's word was 'The Covenant'. Ours
'The Lord of Hosts'. There was a very hot dispute
at swords' point between our horse and theirs. At
the push of pike we did repel the stoutest
regiment the Enemy had there. The best of the
horse being broken through in less than an hour,
it became a total rout. We believe about 3000
were slain. Thus you have one of the most signal
mercies God hath done for England.

Charles II attempted to stir English Royalists to
support him by taking a Scottish army south: at
Worcester in 1651 Cromwell caught up with him and
destroyed his force. Charles escaped abroad.
Cromwell was now able to end Covenanting rule. It
had become very strict indeed, for the Covenanters
insisted people had to go to Church and no-one who
had ever helped the royal cause could hold an official
post. They also excluded anyone:

G . . . given to uncleanness, bribery, swearing,
drunkenness or deceiving, or scandalous in their
conversation, or who neglect their worship of
God in their families.

Cromwell ended such rules and merged Scotland
with England: he stationed several thousand English
troops in bases at Leith, Inverness and other key
points. At last a kind of peace settled upon the
country.

1 Do you think the author of source C was a
supporter of Montrose? Explain your
answer.
2 This is a confusing period. Design a
simple diagram called 'The main steps to
Union' that will explain these events to
someone who knows nothing about them.

THE RETURN OF STEWART RULE

A *Charles II*

In 1658 Oliver Cromwell died. There was no-one able to replace him so, in 1660, Charles II returned to be warmly welcomed by many people in England and Scotland. Charles spent his time in England, and left Scottish affairs in the hands of the Earl of Lauderdale who, according to a writer of the time:

B Made a very ill appearance. He was very big: his hair was red, hanging loosely about him: his whole manner was very rough and boisterous and very unfit for a court.

Once more England and Scotland became separate states that shared the same King. A small number of the King's enemies were arrested and executed, including the Duke of Argyll. Charles and Lauderdale were determined to control Scotland. This meant, once again, tackling the big issue of religious beliefs and how the Kirk was organised. The King declared that Acts of Parliament passed since 1633 were all cancelled. These had set up a Scottish Church that was outside royal control. Instead, in 1662, there came a new law (**C**):

C His Majesty, with the consent of his parliament, has thought it necessary, and do hereby restore the bishops to their ancient places and privileges in parliament, and all their other privileges, abolishing acts by which the sole power within the church stands with general assemblies, presbyteries and kirk sessions.

The General Assembly of the Kirk no longer met, and bishops helped the King control the Kirk. The system of choosing ministers for each parish was also changed as Lauderdale restored the way of working that had operated under James VI. Each minister had to be approved by a bishop and by the main landowner in the area. Many people were ready to accept these changes, but a very determined group were not. About a third of all ministers – around 270 in number – left the Kirk rather than agree to the changes. They were especially numerous in the south-west where they had strong support from local people.

In the following years first Lauderdale, and then (after he had failed) the King's Roman Catholic brother, James, Duke of York, struggled to find a way of dealing with these people. They saw these remaining Covenanters as enemies who would not accept royal government and, after all the upheavals of the age of Cromwell, this is not surprising. The names given to these Covenanters vary: sometimes they are called 'Whigs' and sometimes 'Cameronians' (after one of their early leaders, Richard Cameron). In June 1680 a declaration by a leading Cameronian stated:

D We, as representatives of the true Presbyterian Kirk, do disown Charles Stewart that has been reigning (or rather tyrannising) on the throne of Britain, as having any right to the crown of Scotland. We, being under the standard of Our Lord Jesus Christ, do declare war with such a tyrant. We disown and resent the reception of the Duke of York, that papist, as against our principles.

The clash between Covenanters like the Cameronians and the Government, involved violence. Government forces tried to prevent the Covenanters holding services in private houses, or in the open air. In 1679 a group of nine Covenanters stopped the coach of one of their leading enemies, James Sharp, Archbishop of St Andrews. Before the horrified gaze of Sharp's daughter, Isabella, they killed the Archbishop. Only two of the murderers were eventually caught and executed.

E *The murder of Archbishop Sharp*

The Government sent 9000 troops to the south-west to try and stamp out the Covenanting movement. Most were Highlanders and a writer of the time noted:

F **They carried away a great many horses and no small quantity of goods out of merchants' shops, linen and woollen cloth and some silver plate. You should have seen them, loaded down with bedclothes, carpets, clothes, pots, pans, shoes and furniture.**

Laws were made harsher. Preaching at an illegal gathering became punishable by death. The Government's actions made Covenanters arm themselves. One armed group even threatened Glasgow, and the King's illegitimate son, the Duke of Monmouth, had to be called north to lead an army against them. At Bothwell Bridge his force of 10 000 defeated the 4000-strong Covenanters and sent around 200 to go and live in exile in the West Indies. Their ship sank off Orkney and most drowned.

In 1681 the Government brought in a new law, the Test Act. This required all who held any sort of official post to swear to support the King's power over Government and the Kirk. Hunting down Covenanters continued. One of those leading the hunt was John Graham of Claverhouse. He was so enthusiastic about this work that he even left his bride on his wedding day in order to carry on with it. The numbers

G *Covenanters being arrested*

(around 100) who were executed in 1685 earned this period the name of 'The Killing Time'. **G** shows Edinburgh Covenanters being led away to be punished.

In 1685 Charles II died. The new King, his brother James, was a Roman Catholic who at once began promoting Catholics to important positions. Holyrood Abbey became a Catholic chapel. James's actions caused even more alarm in England than in Scotland. At first most of his enemies were content to wait for James to die, for his successor would be his Protestant daughter Mary. Mary had married a Dutchman, William, Prince of Orange and the Dutch court had become a place of refuge for Scottish and English opponents of James. But in June 1688, James's second wife gave birth to a son. Leading people in England decided to invite Mary and William to replace James. As William landed in England, James panicked and fled.

Few Lowland Scots regretted the departure of James VII, nor did some of the Highland clans – especially the Campbells. But John Graham (now Viscount Dundee) was able to raise a force of MacDonalds, Stewarts, Camerons and Macleans, to fight for James. His army was met on 25 July 1689 by a force of Lowland Scots led by General Hugh Mackay in the narrow pass of Killiecrankie. The ferocious Highland charge proved too much for Mackay's men, who were defeated and fled. Graham, however, was struck by a bullet as he charged, and died. His army pushed south only to be blocked by a Covenanting force at Dunkeld. This force was much smaller than the Highland army, but it was made up of the followers of Richard Cameron, the Covenanter who had died for his beliefs in 1680. Their leader, William Cleland, died in the battle, but the psalm-singing Cameronians proved to be too determined for their opponents. The Highland army retreated and, after a further defeat at Cromdale in 1690, abandoned the war and returned to their homes. William went on to crush James VII's Irish supporters in the Battle of the Boyne.

1 Why did the new law (C) cause so much trouble?

2 How did the authors of source D justify declaring war on the King?

3 Why would the Test Act have angered Covenanters?

4 Use source G and information in this section to make up the page of a diary of a Covenanter who saw these events taking place.

GLENCOE

William and Mary's Government had defeated the armies that fought for James VII. But they wished to feel they were in full control of the country. The most troublesome part of it was the Highlands. It was Highlanders who made up Dundee's army at Killiecrankie and the Government suspected that many Highland chiefs still thought of James as their true King. At first the Government tried to win over these chiefs. The Earl of Breadalbane was given £12 000 to hand out to them. What exactly happened to this money has never been entirely clear but it did not seem to solve the problem. A military stronghold was developed at Fort William (where once Cromwell's soldiers had been based). Its commander, Colonel Hill, had several thousand soldiers to deal with trouble. Government troops included a new regiment, the first Highland Regiment in the British Army. It was raised by the Earl of Argyll (head of the Campbell clan) and named after him. But still the Government did not feel safe. King William was eager to use all the soldiers that Britain could provide in his wars with the Catholic King of France, Louis XIV. He had to feel secure at home. In September 1691 he issued a proclamation (**A**).

A We pardon and forgive all that have been in arms against us of all treason, rebellion, and robberies upon this condition: that the persons shall swear and sign the oath of allegiance [loyalty] to us by the first day of January next. Such as continue obstinate after this gracious offer of mercy shall be punished as traitors and rebels.

B *Master of Stair*

William did not come north, but left it to Sir John Dalrymple, Master of Stair, his chief minister in Scotland, to carry out his plan. Stair was a Lowland Scot who was very suspicious indeed of Highland people and their ways.

Stair decided that strong action had to be taken against the clans that did not sign the oath. Like many government supporters, he especially disliked the MacDonalds. The large Clan Donald lived in many groups, one being the Macdonalds of Glencoe under their elderly chief Alasdair MacDonald, the 12th Maclain of Glencoe. MacDonalds had fought for Charles I, Charles II and James VII. They were bitter enemies of the pro-Government Campbells who followed the Earl of Argyll. They also had a long record of raiding their neighbours: the MacDonalds of Glencoe, returning from the Battle of Killiecrankie, had gone into the Campbell lands of Glenlyon and taken away everything that they could steal, leaving the people little to live on. Stair wrote:

C I think the Clan Donald must be rooted out. Since we will make them desperate I think we should root them out before they can get the help they depend on. Those that lay down their arms (weapons) at King James's command will take them up at his orders.

He also believed:

D The winter time is the only season in which we are sure the Highlanders cannot escape and carry their wives, bairns, and cattle to the hills. This is the proper time to maul them in the long, dark nights.

Many clan chiefs would not sign the oath to King William until James VII gave permission. He did not do this until 12 December 1691, and news of it took several days to reach Scotland. Nevertheless, by 1 January 1692 they had all signed but two. One of them, Glengarry, was a powerful chief with a stronghold that troops would not easily capture. When he eventually signed the oath, several days late, it was accepted. This left the MacDonalds of Glencoe. Stair wrote to Sir Thomas Livingstone, military commander in Scotland:

E I am glad that Glencoe did not come in within the time prescribed. I think to harry [kill and steal] their cattle or burn their houses is but to make them desperate lawless men to rob their neighbours, but I believe you will be satisfied it were a great advantage to the nation that thieving tribe were rooted out and cut off.

In fact Maclain took the oath five days late as a result of first going to the wrong place (Fort William instead of Inverary), being held up by dreadful weather, and finding the sheriff away when he finally arrived. He was allowed to take the oath after breaking down, weeping and pleading on behalf of his people. He returned home believing he had saved them. A few days later red-coated soldiers arrived. Their commander was Captain Robert Campbell of

Glenlyon, a 60-year-old who had almost ruined himself through drink and gambling. He explained that Fort William was too crowded for his men and they were to stay in Glencoe. The MacDonalds made them welcome, each house taking two or three men. In fact he was there for quite different reasons. His troops were part of Argyll's Regiment of Foot commanded by Major Robert Duncanson: many of them were Campbells. After two weeks, on 12 February, their orders arrived from Duncanson:

> **F** **You are hereby ordered to fall upon the rebels the MacDonalds of Glencoe and put all to the sword under 70 [years old]. You are to have special care that the Old Fox and his sons do upon no account escape. This you are to put into execution at 5 o'clock in the morning precisely. This is by the King's special command for the good and safety of the country. See that this is put into execution else you may be expected to be treated as a man not true to the King or Government.**

Duncanson moved to block escape from the Glen with the rest of the regiment. His own orders had stated that the killing should start at 7.00 am. Robert Campbell's soldiers carried out their task, 38 MacDonalds were killed, including Maclain, who was struggling to dress. But the chief's sons escaped, as did many more, for a very severe snowstorm covered their flight. Several more died from the cold.

A commission enquired into the massacre, called it 'a barbarous murder' and stated that Stair had gone beyond his orders. Parliament, too, blamed Stair and declared that his soldiers had greatly offended by attacking the very people who were looking after them. They were guilty of 'slaughter under trust'. But no-one was punished, though Stair lost his position as chief minister in Scotland. Nor did the Campbells of Glenlyon and the MacDonalds of Glencoe become bitter enemies – in fact they fought side by side in the Jacobite cause early in the next century.

H *The Pass of Glencoe*

G *Robert Campbell of Glenlyon*

Clan members lived in hiding until, eventually, Colonel Hill got permission for them to return. As news of the massacre spread, so leading people involved claimed they were innocent. Robert Campbell explained:

> **I** **I had several orders from London and also several orders from the Commander-in-Chief and all extraordinary strict to destroy these people and take no prisoners.**

1 Duncanson altered the time of the attack. No-one really knows why. What do you think?

2 Robert Campbell died in 1696, his last years made miserable by the Glencoe Massacre. Do you think he should have disobeyed his orders?

3 Look at source E. Why did Stair think it was necessary to be so brutal?

4 How might a MacDonald who escaped have described these events, many years later, to a young relative?

WHAT SORT OF SCOTLAND NOW?

The King of Scotland had fled. Those who supported him had been defeated. This left three questions to be sorted out.

1 What sort of Kirk was going to be set up?

2 What sort of Government was going to be set up?

3 Would England and Scotland be linked together? If so, how closely?

A *King William*

The people of Scotland were not agreed about any of these questions. Ordinary people were not asked what they thought. Such matters were decided by powerful people who first met in March 1689 at a special gathering of the Scottish Parliament called a Convention. Since the members still feared attack from supporters of James, they met behind locked doors, guarded by 1000 Cameronians. James's supporters left, and the bishops declared they supported James, so that left decisions in the hands of those who favoured both a kirk free of royal control and bishops, and a Parliament with more power. The Parliament voted to take the crown from James VII. In early April 1689, it produced two statements, one called the Claim of Right, the other the Articles of Grievances. In them Parliament declared:

B

- No Roman Catholic could be monarch or could hold an official position.
- No monarch could overrule the law.
- Parliament had to meet often.
- Taxes had to have Parliament's agreement.
- Bishops were condemned.

Parliament offered William the crown: William accepted, becoming William II of Scotland and III of England. In 1690 the General Assembly of the Kirk met once more. William favoured tolerating different religious beliefs, but since the bishops supported James he could not resist the Assembly when it decided to end the power of bishops, to reject any idea that the monarch was head of the Kirk, and to require the General Assembly to meet once a year.

Ministers who did not agree to these decisions were generally removed from their positions, though (in the north-east especially) it took many years. The Church of Scotland was to be a presbyterian church. Those who favoured keeping bishops built up their own 'episcopal' church instead.

William did not come to Scotland but left it to others to manage affairs. When he died in March 1702, his wife was already dead, and he was succeeded by her sister, Anne. Anne reigned until 1714, but throughout her life the question of who should succeed her loomed large. She gave birth to 18 children but 17 of them died in infancy or were stillborn: her son William survived 11 years but died in 1700. Should the son of James VII (James died in 1701) be allowed to return to succeed Anne? He was a Catholic and spent much of his time with England's enemy, Louis XIV of France. The English Parliament passed a law in 1701, called the Act of Settlement, which stated that James was not acceptable. Instead the English crown was to go to a descendant of James VI, Sophia, Protestant ruler of the small German state of Hanover. Should Scotland do the same? This question became tied up with the attitude of Scots towards England, and events after 1689 had made some Scots hostile.

The main cause of Scottish anger was the failure of an attempt to set up a colony at Darien in central America.

1 Were the Scots right to blame England for the failure of the Darien colony? Look through the evidence and decide.
2 How might the Spanish governor of a nearby colony have described these events?

This was a time when big efforts were being made to increase Scottish wealth. In 1695 the Bank of Scotland was set up. The same year saw the founding of the Company of Scotland. An Act of Parliament stated:

C This Company is empowered to equip and navigate their ships to any lands in Asia, Africa, or America and there to plant colonies, build cities or forts in places not inhabited, or by the

consent of the natives and not possessed by any European State, and by force of arms to defend their trade and colonies.

D *A map of Darien drawn in 1699*

The English East India Company was alarmed by this rival organisation: it used its power to stop English people and Dutch and German financiers from putting money into the Company of Scotland. But Scots invested heavily, finding £400 000 in six months and so making possible the purchase of a small fleet. The Company decided to create a colony on a narrow strip of land in the Panama area of Central America. They had a map, provided by Lionel Wafer, an Englishman who had been there (**D**). However, little notice was taken of Wafer's comments on the hot and wet climate in the area. A key figure in these affairs was a London-based Scot, William Paterson, who had made a fortune in the West Indies trade: when an expedition for Darien finally set sail in 1698, Paterson and his wife were on board.

Attempts at founding Scottish colonies had already failed in New Jersey (1682) and South Carolina (1684); the Darien expedition was entering territory that was seen by the Spanish government as part of its empire. The five ships carried 1200 seamen and colonists and cargoes for trading that included Bibles, wigs and heavy woollen cloth. According to two survivors of the expedition, once they'd landed:

E **For near about two months before they came away, officers, seamen and planters were seized with a severe sickness. Near about 200 died. Their sickness happened through want of provisions. They spent their time there mostly in fortifying and building.**

Among the victims of sickness was William Paterson's wife. Faced with the problems of living in a fever swamp, and refused help from the nearby English colony of Jamaica, the remaining colonists left. A further expedition, however, had been preparing to join the first group and set sail from the Clyde on the very day that news arrived of the return of the *Caledonia*, the one surviving vessel from the first expedition. One of the new colonists, Henrietta Tayler, wrote on 28 February 1700:

F **You would best imagine how melancholy and disappointing it was to us when we expected that all was in a flourishing condition, to find an entire desertion. I wish to God we may surmount the difficulties and that a regular way may be found for our subsistence [food] till such time as we can do it for ourselves. If that be done that colony will prosper yet and in time not only repay the vast charges the kingdom has been at but also enrich us so that we may be known in the world as a nation.**

The colonists had to fight off a Spanish attack and endure a Spanish naval blockade until life became unbearable and they too left on 12 April 1700. Only one of the three ships returned safely. Further Company of Scotland ships had mixed fortunes: one successful trade-trip to Africa brought back gold and ivory, while another led to disaster as pirates seized and burned the vessel. These were severe setbacks for a small country that was already hit by a whole series of bad harvests between 1695 and 1701. In these years around 5 per cent of Scotland's population actually died of starvation. Moreover, Scotland was drawn into England's wars with Louis XIV. Scottish soldiers fought abroad, and taxes placed on Scotland helped to pay for the wars. It was against these events that the Scottish Parliament drew up the Act of Security (1704), refusing to automatically accept the Act of Settlement passed in England. The English Parliament replied with the Aliens Act (1705) threatening to treat Scots as foreigners if they refused to agree to the Hanoverian succession. This would have seriously hurt exports of cattle, sheep, coal, linen and other goods. The captain and two of the crew of the English ship *Worcester* suffered the results of Scottish anger. Despite lack of evidence they were hanged in Edinburgh for being pirates. Union between the two countries seemed a long way off.

UNION

On 16 January 1707 the members of the Scottish Parliament voted, by a majority of 43, to abolish themselves. They decided to agree to the Act of Union, which stated:

A That the two kingdoms of England and Scotland shall, upon the first day of May 1707, and for ever after, be united into one kingdom by the name of Great Britain, the crosses of St George and St Andrew [will] be conjoined and used in all flags.

That the United Kingdom of Great Britain be represented by one and the same Parliament.

That all the subjects of the United Kingdom shall have full freedom of trade to and from any place within the United Kingdom and the Dominions.

This was a remarkable event for two countries that had quarrelled so often in the past. Ever since James VI became King of England too the idea of a union between the two countries had often been discussed. The rulers in London were often especially interested in a union, for they did not find it very easy to manage Scotland too. But why should the members of the Scottish Parliament agree? One Scottish noble, the Earl of Roxburgh, suggested in 1705 that if union did come about:

B The motives will be, trade with most, Hanover with some, ease and security with others, together with a general aversion [dislike] to civil discords, intolerable poverty and the constant oppression of a bad ministry.

It is easy to see why English rulers wanted union. They desired peace and safety inside the country at a time of war with France. They wanted to be sure that when Queen Anne died, the next ruler would be Protestant, not a Catholic member of the Stewart family. The Queen herself was keen to see union come about and sent the young John Campbell, Duke of Argyll, to persuade the Scottish Parliament to discuss the union. Argyll was successful – 31 Scottish commissioners, led by the Duke of Queensberry, travelled to London to start talks with 31 English commissioners. Only one of the Scots was an opponent of union, for the Queen had been allowed to choose them. The two sides met in separate rooms, passing each other messages in writing. In this way they agreed the terms of the Act of Union (**C**).

C

- There was to be just one parliament for the whole of the united country.
- English standards of weights and measures and coinage would apply to Scotland too.
- Scotland was to keep its own laws and education system.
- Scotland was to receive £385 085 to help it clear its debts and share in the debts of the English government: the money was also to help compensate people who had supported the Darien scheme.
- Scotland was to send 45 MPs to join the 513 English MPs. Thirty were to be chosen by wealthy people in the counties and 15 by the royal burghs, meeting in districts. Scottish nobles were to choose 16 of their number to join the House of Lords.
- There was to be a seven-year period before the English salt and malt taxes applied to Scotland too.

This plan was soon approved by the English Parliament; the Scottish Parliament debated it for ten weeks before finally accepting it. Most of the nobles in the Scottish Parliament were strongly in favour of it, but other members were less sure. The Kirk was not eager to merge with an English Parliament in which bishops were important members of the House of Lords. A special Bill of Security was therefore drawn up promising to leave the Kirk alone. Parliament did not represent ordinary people and in the streets of Edinburgh and Glasgow there were protests that were sometimes violent. Queensberry was very unpopular and went in fear of attack. During discussions the union was attacked by men like Andrew Fletcher of Saltoun and Lord Belhaven. Belhaven said:

D When I consider the treaty, I see the English constitution remaining firm, the same two houses of parliament, the same taxes, the same customs and excise . . . and all ours subject to either regulations or annihilations only we have the honour to pay their debts.

But others argued that the union would mean peace, an end to dangerous quarrels, and a chance to trade more fully with both England and the English empire. Around £20 000 was used to help win over support (though much went to men who would have supported it anyway). A supporter of union argued:

G *Queen Anne receiving the Treaty*

E This nation, being poor and without force to protect its commerce, cannot reap great advantage by it till it partake of the trade and protection of some powerful neighbour nation.

At a key point in voting, the leader of the opposition to union, the Duke of Hamilton, stayed away, claiming that he had toothache. His behaviour has always seemed rather puzzling to historians. The Treaty was finally accepted, therefore, and the Scottish Parliament met for the last time on 25 March 1707. Queen Anne was delighted, declaring:

F I desire and expect from all my subjects of both nations that henceforth they act with all possible respect and kindness to one another, that so it may appear to all the world they have hearts to become one people.

Yet only six years later, Scots nobles who supported the union were arguing that it should be ended, and a vote to bring this about failed to pass the House of Lords by just four votes. For union did not seem to fulfil the hopes of many of its Scottish supporters. The Kirk was angry that an Act of Toleration in 1712 allowed the Episcopalians the right to worship freely (as long as they prayed for the reigning monarch). It also hated another law of the same year that ended the system of 1690 by which each church congregation chose its minister: now powerful owners of land appointed ministers. Some Scots businesses soon profited from union, others suffered from English competition, whilst high taxes were a widespread grumble. Robert Wodrow, a Scot who lived through these years, wrote in 1724:

H Under this peace we are growing much worse. The poverty and debts of many are increasing. Trade is much failed, the run of our nobility and gentry to England, their wintering there and educating their children there takes away a vast deal of money.

The way was open for members of the Stewart family who lived abroad but still claimed to be the rightful rulers, to stir up trouble for the union government in London.

1 Look carefully at source B.
   a Explain it in your own words.
   b Do you think that Roxburgh has mentioned all the main reasons for the union of parliaments?
2 Look at source E. Do you agree with what this person said?
3 Supporters of the return of the Catholic James Stewart tried to win more support. Design the kind of poster that they might have produced.

THREATS TO THE GOVERNMENT IN THE EARLY 1700s

James VII and II had fled from Britain in 1688. In 1701 he died. His son, James Edward, now claimed that he was the rightful ruler. Those who supported him were known as 'Jacobites' (since the Latin word for James is 'Jacobus'). But when Queen Anne died she was succeeded not by James Edward, but by the ruler of the little German state of Hanover: he was proclaimed King George I in Edinburgh on 5 August 1714. In this way Scotland had to accept the Act of Settlement that had been passed by the English Parliament before the Union, for English leaders were determined to have a Protestant King. Several Scottish leaders gathered around the new King in the hope of winning his favour. One of these was John Erskine, Earl of Mar, who was one of the men who had carried through the union of parliaments. But Mar found that the new King and his ministers had no time for him, and that he had to give up his government post. When a letter from James Edward arrived, asking Mar to raise support for the Jacobite cause, he disguised himself as a workman, sailed north, and prepared to lead a rising against the Government.

Many other people in Scotland were far from happy with what had happened since 1707 and with their new rulers. In the north-east especially, these feelings of resentment were particularly strong, as well as continuing loyalty to the Stewart family. Some Highland clan chiefs, too, were ready to fight, whilst there were hopes that English Jacobites would support the rising. But there was little chance of powerful help from abroad: in 1714, that great friend of the Jacobites, King Louis XIV of France, died and his successor had no time for risky adventures. Nevertheless, on 6 September at Braemar, Mar declared that James Edward was the true king and raised the standard, the flag to mark the great event (rather worryingly, the golden ball on the flagpole fell off). Armed men came in support and Mar soon had 12 000 followers. He marched on Perth and occupied the town.

Mar was not a skilful commander. He waited for many weeks even though the Duke of Argyll's government force, which blocked his way south, was far smaller than the Jacobite army. Mar chose to detach 2000 of his men under Mackintosh of Borlum; this force marched south and joined Scots Borderers under Lord Kenmure and English Borderers commanded by Lord Derwentwater. They were persuaded by the leader of the English Jacobites, Thomas Forster, to advance into Lancashire where many folk were thought to be Jacobites. But, at Preston, they were trapped and surrounded by a larger government army to which they eventually surrendered.

This episode happened at the very same time as Mar had at last stirred himself into action. At Sheriffmuir, near Stirling, his soldiers fought the smaller army led by the Duke of Argyll in a confusing and indecisive battle. The right wing of Mar's force charged their enemies and defeated them: but the left wing was forced to reel back before a fierce attack from Argyll's cavalry. It was now mid-November 1715, and some of Mar's Highlanders began to drift home, whilst fresh troops arrived to swell the size of Argyll's force. A Jacobite report put the best face possible on the battle:

A **We compute that here lay killed upon the field of battle about seven or eight hundred of the enemy, and though we cannot make an exact account of their loss, yet this is certain, that there lay dead upon the field above fifteen of the enemy to one of ours. The prisoners taken by us were very civilly used and none of them stripped. The few prisoners taken by the enemy were most of them stripped, and some wounded after being taken.**

B *The arrival of James Edward*

James Edward arrived at Peterhead in late December to join a campaign that was going badly. He did not make a good impression on one Jacobite, who described his leader thus:

C **His person was tall and thin. His countenance [face] was pale. His speech was**

grave . . . but his words were few . . . Neither can I say I ever saw him smile. We saw nothing in him that looked like spirit. He never appeared with cheerfulness and vigour to animate us. Our men began to despise him: some asked if he could speak. His countenance looked extremely heavy.

The would-be King was extremely gloomy. He said:

D For me it is no new thing to be unfortunate since my whole life from my cradle has been a constant series of misfortunes.

At Montrose he abandoned his diminishing army and, with Mar, set sail for France. The rest of the Jacobite force faded away back to their homes. The victorious Government had two Jacobite leaders, Derwentwater and Kenmure, beheaded.

E *Execution of the Earl of Derwentwater and Viscount Kenmure in 1716*

Twenty-two Jacobites were hanged at Preston and hundreds punished by being transported to work in the plantations. The Government tried to disarm the clans but only loyal clans genuinely parted with their weapons. It also seized the lands of leading Jacobites. But few clansmen were ready to rally to a fresh attempt at a rising that took place in 1719, when 307 Spanish troops came with Jacobite leaders and wandered inland until caught at Glenshiel. The Spanish troops were sent home.

The Government was still far from being in firm control of Scotland. It relied especially on the Duke of Argyll and his brother to help rule the country, but the Campbell clan led by these two was not popular with many Highlanders. In fact, during the 1715 rising, a gathering of Macleans and MacDonalds had tried to capture the Campbell stronghold at Inverary. When the Government tried to make Scots pay the

F *Ruthven Barracks*

high tax on malt that was already being paid in England, there was a great deal of anger. This led to further attempts to control the country.

Major General George Wade was appointed in 1725 as Commander-in-Chief of Scotland. He began a programme of building forts and barracks, linking them together with military roads along which soldiers and supplies could move speedily. Wade's work resulted in 260 miles (420 km) of roads and many bridges: a further 830 miles (1330 km) were added by his successor William Caulfield. Also in 1725, clan chiefs in certain areas were allowed to raise six companies of men to form a 'watch' to stop cattle stealing. (In 1739 these soldiers formed a unit in the regular army that came to be known as the 'Black Watch' because of the dark-coloured tartan that they wore.) In 1727 money was provided to allow a Board of Trustees to assist industry and fisheries in Scotland. These actions, it was hoped, would help secure peace.

1 Read source A.
a How has its Jacobite author tried to describe his side in the most favourable way?
b What else would you need to know before you could believe that source A is accurate?
2 Read source C. Do you blame James Edward for being like this? Do you think he should have behaved differently?
3 You have to explain to someone who has never studied the period, just why the 1715 rising failed. What would you say?

THE 1745 UPRISING

A *The sea battle between* Lion *and* Elizabeth

In 1745 Britain and France were at war. On 9 July Captain Brett of the 58-gun warship HMS *Lion* saw two French warships, the 64-gun *Elizabeth* and the 16-gun *Du Teillay*. He engaged them in an action (**A**) that left both the *Lion* and the *Elizabeth* badly damaged and forced to return to their home ports. The *Du Teillay* sailed on. Had Captain Brett but known it he might have concentrated on her for she carried the 25-year-old Prince Edward Stewart who was sailing for Scotland to try to stir up an uprising that would make his father the King.

B *Prince Charles*

The Prince was a good-looking, determined and very persuasive man. He needed to be, for when he landed on 23 July on Eriskay he brought with him but around a dozen followers and a small supply of weapons. Local chiefs expected a good deal more than this if they were to risk an uprising. Yet the Prince was able to argue that even though he had not brought a French army with him, Scotland was very badly defended by Government troops. Most were on the continent, leaving small numbers scattered around, many of them being new recruits. When the important clan chief, Donald Cameron of Lochiel, Chief of the Clan Cameron, arrived, the Prince won him over, declaring:

C **In a few days with a few friends I will erect the royal standard and proclaim to the people of Britain that Charles Stewart is come over to claim the crown of his ancestors, to win it or to perish in the attempt. Lochiel, who, my father told me, was our firmest friend, may stay at home and learn from the newspapers the fate of his prince.**

According to an English soldier, Captain Edward Burt, who was in the Highlands at the time:

D **The ordinary Highlanders love their Chief and pay him a blind obedience, although it be in opposition to the Government; they say they ought to do whatever he commands without enquiry.**

In fact, if clansmen sometimes did not wish to be drawn into dangerous events, then they faced threats like these made by Lochiel's followers to some of the clan:

E **They went from house to house and made clear to all the Camerons that if they forthwith did not go along with them they would that instant proceed to burn all their houses and cripple their cattle.**

On 19 August Charles was able to raise his standard in front of around 900 Camerons and MacDonalds at Glenfinnan (**H**). As General Cope struggled to pull together Government forces, Charles's Jacobite army was able to make excellent use of Wade's military roads to reach Perth on 4 September. There he was joined by further supporters including his most able military commander, and a former regular soldier, Lord George Murray. By 16 September the force had reached Edinburgh where it was able to rush the open gates and take control of the city. It did not, however, have the artillery to force the castle to surrender. Charles had swept through the Highlands at a time when many people lived half-starved lives and hated the Government. Not only Roman Catholics, but Episcopalians (like Lochiel) were attracted to his cause. But leading noblemen stood aside, many towns of the south did not care for this threat to their peaceful lives, the Presbyterian Church was hostile, and clans like the Campbells as well as others in the far north, were all determined enemies.

General Cope's forces had failed to intercept Charles further north, but they now took ship from Aberdeen to Dunbar and marched to Prestopans. Here, on 21 September, they faced the Jacobite force. The numbers of each army – around 2000 – were similar. Cope had cavalry and artillery but both units were new recruits unused to battle. The Highlanders' method of fighting was designed to terrify an enemy. Sir John Dalrymple, writing in 1771, looked back:

F Their arms were a broadsword, a dagger called a dirk, a targe (a round shield), a musket, and two pistols. In battle they threw off the plaid, making their movements quicker. Their advance was rapid. When near the enemy they stopped a little to draw breath and discharge their muskets which they then dropped on the ground. Advancing, they fired their pistols and then rushed into the enemy ranks with the broadsword, threatening and shaking the sword as they ran.

This fearsome sight terrified Cope's gunners and cavalrymen, who promptly fled. The battle was over in 15 minutes. The Irish Jacobite John William O'Sullivan, one of Charles's leading officers, wrote:

G Sullivan cried out 'Let the MacDonalds come to this hedge, we have out-winged them': the Dragoons, hearing this, made a motion, upon which Sullivan cried out 'Let the first rank fire', which they did: the Dragoons went off as fast as they could ride. The left, composed of Camerons, Stewarts and MacGregors, rushed in with such fury upon the enemy after their first discharge, that they had no time to discharge their cannon, and then the broadswords played their part for, with one stroke, arms and legs were cut off and heads split open to the shoulders.

H

Charles still lacked control of parts of Scotland, but was determined to press on. A Government army under Marshall Wade waited at Newcastle; Charles therefore led his army south-west, taking Carlisle and passing through Preston and Manchester onwards to Derby. From there it was but 130 miles (210 km) to London: the Prince was eager to continue. But Lord George Murray and the other army leaders opposed him. From 4 to 6 December they argued their case that further advance was foolish. Only 200–300 English Jacobites had joined them. No sizeable French force had arrived, and British regular troops were returning from the Continent, together with Dutch and German soldiers. This meant that Wade, and King George II's young son, the Duke of Cumberland, commanded forces far bigger than the Jacobite army. The Prince had to agree to a retreat.

By 19 December the Jacobites were once more passing through Carlisle, and on Christmas Day they reached Glasgow. There they found that people were hostile. On 17 January they were able to defeat the pursuing Government army led by Henry Hawley, yet remained at risk in southern Scotland. Lord George Murray, Lochiel, and the other army leaders wrote to the Prince:

I A vast number of soldiers are gone home since the Battle of Falkirk. We are of the opinion that there is no way out of the danger but retiring immediately to the Highlands. The hard marches which your army have undergone, and the winter season, cannot fail of making this measure approved of.

The Jacobites pulled back to the Inverness area. In slow pursuit up to Aberdeen came a large force of experienced soldiers led by the King's son who was eager for revenge. At Aberdeen, Cumberland's men trained for the coming battle in the spring of 1746.

1 Using information in this section and the next, make up a time-line of the events of this uprising.
2 Using the information and an atlas, make up a sketch map of the Jacobite route during these events.
3 Why do you think Lochiel was so persuaded by the Prince (source C)?
4 Look at sources F and G. How might General Cope have excused his defeat.

CULLODEN, 1746

Alexander Carlyle, a Scots visitor to London, was sitting in one of the new coffee houses with a friend, when:

A **. . . news of the Battle of Culloden arrived and London all over was in a perfect uproar of joy. The mob were so riotous that we were glad to take our swords from our belts and walk with them in our hands. Smollett cautioned me against speaking a word lest the mob should discover my country.**

The battle took place in chilly, grey and windy weather on Drumossie Muir on 16 April. It began at 1.00 pm: by 2.00 pm the Jacobite army had been broken, and those that could, fled from the battlefield. Prince Charles fled too, all his hopes finally destroyed. The battle marked the end of Jacobite ambitions.

Why did the Jacobites lose?
1 Read source B, which was written by Lord George Murray the day after the battle. What reasons does Lord George give?
2 Look through the rest of the material in this section. Do you agree with Lord George? Are there other reasons too?

B **It was highly wrong to have set up the royal standard without having positive assurance [promise] from his most Christian Majesty [of France] that he would assist you with all his force. Mr O'Sullivan whom your Royal Highness trusted with the most essential things was exceedingly unfit for it and commanded gross blunders [mistakes]. It was a fatal error to allow the enemy those walls upon their left, flanking in when we went upon the attack. I wish Mr O'Sullivan had never got any other charge [job] in the Army than the care of baggage, his orders were vastly confused. The want of provisions [food] was another misfortune: in the last three days our army was starved. This was the reason for our night march when we might have surprised and defeated the enemy at Nairn, but,**

for want of food, a third of our army was scattered to Inverness and the others who marched had not spirits to make it so quick as was necessary.

In these last days the Prince relied heavily on the advice of John William O'Sullivan rather than listening to Lord George. It was O'Sullivan who decided the battleground and arranged the troops; it was he, too, who argued that the walls to which Lord George referred did not matter.

The Prince led an army of nearly 6000 men. Most were armed with broadswords, dirks, and pistols and muskets. They were brave men who had already shown their fighting skill, but their way of fighting was very different from that followed by regular troops of the time. They were supported by a small force of cavalry and by an artillery unit of 13 quite different guns manned by inexperienced gunners. They were, moreover, tired and hungry. They had just returned from a night march intended to catch the Government force by surprise and, it was hoped, drunk from celebrating their commander's birthday. In fact Cumberland's men were not to be so surprised and no attack was made.

C *Duke of Cumberland*

D *The Battle of Culloden*

The Duke of Cumberland led an army of English and Scots regular troops who were well fed, well equipped and had enjoyed a good night's sleep. Most were experienced soldiers unlikely to panic when attacked, able to stand and fire around four rounds a minute from their muskets. Cumberland had trained them to fight the Jacobite charge by thrusting their bayonets at the man on the right instead of directly ahead. This stopped the Highlanders from being able to ward off the blow with their targe (shield). In **D** the clash of the two sides is shown.

The picture (**D**) was painted by David Morier shortly after the battle, using Jacobite prisoners as models. A large force of cavalry supported the infantry, and so too did an artillery unit skilfully managed by Colonel William Belford. The gunners fired either solid round iron cannonballs or paper containers full of nails and other bits of metal (called 'case' or 'grape') which scattered among an enemy force. Cumberland himself was slightly younger than the prince and was an experienced soldier who was well - regarded by his men. In addition, men from the Campbell clan had arrived to form the Argyll Militia and support the Government in any way they could.

Drumossie Moor gave Cumberland's army several advantages. His infantry and cavalry were able to fire at the enemy over level and open ground. Between Government and Jacobite forces the ground was marshy and likely to slow a Highland charge. The stone walls that ran between the left of Cumberland's force and the right of the Prince's provided shelter for regular troops under Wolfe and the Argyll Militia: from there they could fire into the flank (side) of any Jacobite advance. The shape of the ground and the walls pushed charging Highlanders into one another, stopping all of them from fighting effectively.

The battle opened with an artillery duel. But whereas Jacobite gunners could do little damage, Belford's men sustained a deadly rain of fire. Its impact on the Jacobites was noted by one of Cumberland's men:

F Their lines were formed so thick and deep that the grapeshot made open lanes quite through them, the men dropping down wholesale.

Lord Elcho whose cavalry helped protect the Jacobite retreat, has left this description (**G**) of the battle (**H**):

G Their cannon . . . did great execution. The Highlanders had orders not to move until the word of command was given, and then they were to give their fire very near, draw their swords and

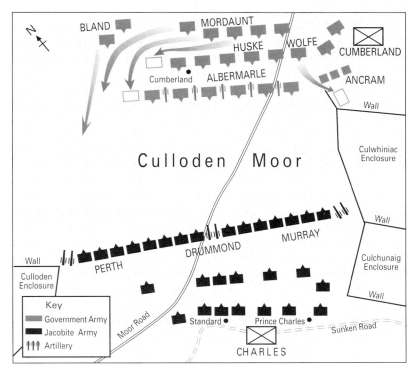

E Plan of the battle

rush in. They suffered the cannonade very impatiently, many threw themselves down flat upon the ground. The Duke's army kept a continuous fire both of cannon and musketry which killed a vast number of the Prince's people.

The Mackintoshes were the first to advance. At last the command to advance was given, and all the line moved forward, but the whole left wing gave way. The centre joined the right and in a sort of mob, broke the regiments opposite to them in the first line, but the second line, marching up, beat them off. As the Campbells had taken possession of the walls they [the Jacobites] received several flank fires which destroyed great numbers. In the attack upon the right many of the Highlanders were killed with bayonets.

Only around 50 Government troops had been killed. Estimates of Jacobite dead vary but were probably around a thousand. Celebrations of the news took place in parts of Scotland: in Glasgow, for example, there was bell-ringing and bonfire-lighting as people expressed their pleasure.

H Programme of events

1.05	Jacobite artillery opens fire.
1.08	Government artillery opens fire and for nearly half an hour Jacobites wait to charge whilst being hit by artillery fire. Wolfe's regiment and Argyll Militia move behind the walls.
1.30	Part of the Highland army charges, led by Mackintoshes, in the face of sustained musket fire.
1.35	This charge hits the left flank of Cumberland's force, pushing back Barrell's regiment, but is stopped and driven off. Other clans charge in vain, pounded by artillery and musket fire from front and side.
1.50	Jacobite retreat. Government cavalry passes through walls broken down for them by the Argyll Militia and attacks the retreating Jacobites, chasing them off the battlefield and killing many.
2.00	Cumberland's army advances and takes control of the battlefield.

AFTER CULLODEN

A large number of armed Jacobites, still ready to fight, began to gather at Ruthven. Many had been coming to join the battle. But plans for further action had not been made: instead the Prince's supporters received a message from their leader:

A **Let every man seek his own safety the best way he can.**

The Prince fled west. Until late September he wandered the Highlands and Western Isles, sheltered by people who were not willing to betray him despite the £30 000 reward for his capture. The most famous of his adventures involved his dressing as a woman, the servant of Flora MacDonald. The Reverend Robert Forbes, a minister of the Episcopal Church, who lived at this time, collected evidence about the Prince (**B**):

B **Miss MacDonald had gone from Skye to South Uist in order to visit her brother. When the Prince was surrounded with difficulties on all hands and knew not what to do for his future safety, Captain O'Neill brought Miss MacDonald to the place where the Prince was and there they concepted the plan. Her step-father was then commander (of Militia forces) she had told him what she was about, upon which he granted a passport for herself, a man servant, and another woman, Betty Burke. Lady Clanranald supplied the Prince with apparel [clothes] for his disguise – a flowered linen gown, a white apron, etc.**

The Prince eventually escaped on a French vessel. Flora MacDonald spent several months in prison for her part in his escape. Charles spent the later part of his life in Rome; a portrait of him at this time (**C**) shows the sadness and disappointment of his life.

He drank very heavily; in 1760 Clementina Walkinshaw, the Scots woman who had lived with him, left him, taking their daughter Charlotte. In 1780 he married a German princess, Louisa, but she too left Charles after one of his especially heavy drinking sessions. He died in 1788, nursed by Charlotte. The role of Jacobite leader now fell to his brother Henry. But Henry was a cardinal in the Roman Catholic Church and had little interest in military adventures – indeed in his last years he accepted a pension from King George III.

Lochiel, wounded at Culloden, escaped to France. Lord George Murray was captured and imprisoned;

C *Charles Edward Stewart in old age*

in later life his views changed and he settled in England. But those Charles left behind suffered cruelly. Many hundreds were arrested and taken down for trial in England. Their leaders were executed either by being hanged, drawn and quartered, or, as in this account (**D**) by the Englishman Horace Walpole, by being beheaded.

D **Then came old Lord Balmerino. As soon as he mounted the scaffold he read the inscription on his coffin. He then surveyed the spectators who were in amazing numbers and pulling out his spectacles, read a treasonable speech. He took the axe and felt it and asked the headsman how many blows he had given Lord Kilmarnock and gave him 3 guineas. Then he put on a nightcap of Scotch plaid and then pulled off his coat and waistcoat and lay down: but being told he was on the wrong side, vaulted round and gave the sign by tossing up his arm.**

Over 900 Jacobites were sent away to the colonies. Those who remained felt the full force of Cumberland's anger. He saw the Jacobites as evil enemies who had to be completely crushed: the '45 had resulted in huge Government forces coming to the Highlands. Duncan Forbes of Culloden, a leading pro-Government Scot who held the position of Lord President of the Court of Session, received all sorts of appeals for help. **E** was sent to him by the magistrates of Inverness.

E **The soldiers generally are the greatest rogues in the British army. They have taken away all the timber that could be found, gates and doors from gardens and all the old houses, even a door of the Church. They have carried off ploughs and plough irons and corn. Our town is reduced to the greatest misery for lack of fire and meal.**

Duncan Forbes protested to Cumberland about the cruelty of his troops, only to be dismissed and described as:

F **That old woman who talked to me of**

G *Fort George*

humanity.

Cumberland left Scotland in mid-July. He received praise and a much increased allowance from a grateful government. But the work of crushing the Highlanders went on under his successor the Earl of Albemarle. Fort Augustus was rebuilt, Fort William strengthened, and garrisons were also put in smaller forts and castles like Corgarff. But, above all, money was poured into the construction of a gigantic new defence, Fort George at Ardersier (**G**).

Raiding parties of soldiers scoured the Highlands with orders like those noted by Colonel Whitefoord:

H Those who are found in arms are ordered to be immediately put to death and the houses of those who abscond [run away] are plundered and burnt and their cattle drove off, their ploughs and other tackle destroyed.

An area where life was already an endless hard struggle was reduced to misery. Troops seized cattle and sold them in thousands to buyers from the south. Naval units cruised off the coast carrying out similar work in coastal places. The illustration **I** was painted in 1884: it shows the artist's view of Jacobite-hunting.

The Government passed laws aimed at preventing such an uprising ever happening again. The lands of leading Jacobites were seized and, until 1784, run by Crown Commissioners. A new Disarming Act (1746) not only denied the Highlanders the right to possess weapons, it also banned the wearing of Highland dress, the use of tartan cloth, and even the playing of bagpipes (Scots units in the army were exempt from these rules). In 1747 the legal powers of clan chiefs were abolished. This hurt pro-Government chiefs

I *Troops hunting Jacobites*

like the Duke of Argyll too, but they were paid compensation. Many Jacobites had been Episcopalians: the Episcopalian clergy were therefore required to swear a new oath of loyalty to the King and had to pray publicly for the royal family. The recruiting of Highlanders was seen, too, as a way of drawing off their fighting skill. In 1751 the Secretary for War said:

J I am for having in our army as many Scottish soldiers as possible because they are generally more hardy and less mutinous, and of all Scots soldiers I would choose to have as many Highlanders as possible.

Life among Highland landowners began to change. A writer in the late 1700s looked back to this time and wrote:

K Even the gentry who had not been engaged in the rebellion found it wise to drop some of their national customs, which either gave offence or were prohibited by law. Their successors have no longer the same attachment either to their people or the ancient ways of life. They copy the

1 Look at C. Compare it with the earlier picture of Charles on page 40. From a study of each, explain how you think the painter saw the Prince. As happy? hopeful? etc.

2 Look at source I. What questions might the soldiers have asked in order to find out whether the people were Jacobites?

3 The events after Culloden earned the Duke of Cumberland the title of 'Butcher'. Why do you think this was? Did he deserve this title?

COUNTRY LIFE FOR ORDINARY PEOPLE

Throughout this time most ordinary Scots lived in the countryside, and struggled endlessly to make a living. About three-quarters of the population lived this peasant life. Since photography had not been invented, and these people did not usually write down anything about their lives, how can we find out how they lived?

A, **B** and **C** were drawn by John Slezer, a German who settled in Scotland and travelled the country between 1678 and 1693 making drawings.

A

1 Look through all the sources in this section. Make a list of all the different sorts of sources: label each one as either a 'primary source' or a 'secondary source'.

2 Write down the heading 'Peasant Life'. Under it make a list of all you can find out about their clothes, their homes, their work, their food, etc. Underneath each statement of information show the evidence you have used by completing the sentence 'I know this is true because . . .'

B

C

D is part of a map of Scotland drawn in the mid-1700s. The original is in colour. The dotted (striped) lines show farmland. The little black dots show houses. E was written by the new Laird of Monymusk, describing his property.

E Heath and moor reached up to the gate and the land that was in culture [being farmed], by which their cattle and dung were always at the door. The whole land was raised and uneven and full of stones, many of them very large, and all the ridges crooked in the shape of an S and very high and full of weeds and poor, being worn out with culture. Oats and bear [barley] was the only sort of grain. The farmhouses are all poor dirty huts.

F was written by an English visitor, Thomas Kirke, in 1679.

F The houses of the commonalty [ordinary people] are very mean, mud-wall and thatch the best: but the poorest sort live in such miserable huts as never eye beheld: men, women and children pig together in a poor mousehole of mud, heath and some like matter: in some parts where turf is plentiful they build up little cabins thereof.

G was written by Thomas Morer in 1689. He was an Englishman who was also a church minister serving a Scottish regiment.

G Their harvest is very great of oats and barley, the straw thereof is very serviceable to them for the support of cattle. Not but they have beans, pease and some wheat, but it is oats and

barley on which they chiefly depend. Their fields are open and without fences. Their ordinary women go barefoot, especially in the summer. Yet the husbands have shoes. Their bread, for the most part, is of oatmeal, they make thick cakes called bannocks. Their cheese is not the best, nor butter. The vulgar [ordinary] houses are low and feeble. Their walls are made of a few stones jumbled together without mortar to cement 'em: on which they set up pieces of wood meeting at the top. They cover their houses with turf an inch thick and in the shape of larger tiles which they fasten with wooden pins. 'Tis rare to find chimneys in these places, a small vent (hole) in the roof sufficing to convey the smoke away.

In 1696 the Government made people pay a tax. This led to lists of people being made and H comes from this tax list. It shows the sort of people who lived together at Inver, one of the little clusters of houses (called 'townships') like those shown in D.

H Inver: 6 tenants and their wives, 5 children, 11 male servants [workers] and 3 female servants, 2 shoemakers and wives, 5 cottars [people living in tiny cottages with little scraps of land], 2 weavers and wives, 1 tailor and wife.

I consists of short sections from *A History of the Scottish People 1560–1830*, which was written by the historian T. C. Smout and published in 1969.

I One must imagine the ground everywhere lying as open as moorland, studded with thickets of broom and gorse but unprotected from the sweeping winds by woods . . . The ploughed land was a series of undulating strips or rigs . . . A slope was a drain . . . of the animals of the farm, the plough team were the most essential . . . the beasts might be horses or oxen . . . Even rural families kept at least one dairy cow to provide milk, cheese and butter . . . The peasants themselves were often quite skilled at processing the products of their animals. The men were often passable tanners and shoemakers . . . and could render tallow into candle grease: their wives spun the wool and coloured it but professional weavers usually made it into cloth.

It would be fair to picture the head of the family and his wife sleeping at night in a box bed with their children and servants curled up in their plaids on straw pallets. Apart from the bed, the meal kists, and a stool or two [there was] little furniture.

HIGHLAND LIFE

During this time a special way of life flourished in the Highlands. Visitors from Lowland Scotland, from England, and from other countries, all described it. The '45 uprising helped to end this way of life (though it was slowly changing anyway).

Imagine that you are a visitor from Edinburgh to the Highlands, 300 years ago. Like many travellers, you write down an account of your experiences to show your friends and, perhaps, in the hope of having it published. Think of a suitable title: study the rest of this section carefully before writing your account.

A is a painting which was made in 1660. It shows someone of importance. Study it to work out how the artist has tried to please the man who paid for the painting by making him seem so important. This picture shows one of the men who were so powerful during this period – a Highland chief, the leader of one of the clans in which Highland people were organised. The word 'clan' means 'children'; the chief was the head and 'father' of the clan whose members took the same name as his. The chief divided up the land he controlled, awarding leases of it (or 'tacks') to certain of his clan: these 'tacksmen' then sub-let pieces of their land to clansmen. The clansmen paid rent for the land that they worked and were also expected to fight for the chief when called upon to do so. In return the chief was expected to care for the people of his clan, to protect their interests and look after their needs. The Macneills of Barra, for example, found replacement cows for tenants who lost their animals in winter, and let people who were too old and feeble to work any more stay in their house. During his travels in 1689 Thomas Morer noticed the power of chiefs (**B**) over ordinary people.

A *A Highland chief in 1660*

B They are in great subjection to their lords who have almost an absolute power over 'em. So that when they are summoned they attend them though to the loss of their lives and the little fortune they have.

A large clan gave the clan chief power, for the clan was a fighting unit. **C** shows 'The Laird of Grant's Champion'. It was painted in 1712; even at this date clansmen possessed the kind of weapons shown here and had to turn out to fight for their chief when asked.

C *'The Laird of Grant's Champion'*

Clan chiefs, and their tacksmen, were famous for their kindness to strangers, and for holding great feasts where their pipers played and their bards told stories. The chiefs and their sons were often well-educated men who had travelled away to school and university in Aberdeen or St Andrews, or even France. But even as early as 1521 this Highland way of life seemed odd to a Lowland Scot. John Major described the Highlanders as 'Wild Scots' and their Gaelic language he labelled 'Irish' (**D**).

D One half of Scotland speaks Irish and all these as well as the Islanders we reckon to belong to the Wild Scots. They are more prompt to fight because, born as they are in mountains and dwellers in forests, their very nature is more combative. One part of the Wild Scots have a wealth of cattle, sheep and horses and these, with a thought of the possible loss of their possessions, yield more willing obedience to the courts of law. The other part delight in the chase [hunting] and a life of indolence [laziness], they live upon others and follow their own worthless and savage chief in all courses sooner than pursue an honest industry. War rather than peace is their normal condition. From the mid-leg to the foot they go uncovered, their dress is, for an over-garment, a loose plaid and a shirt.

John Major saw the Highlanders as very warlike. In part this was because of rivalry between clans, but in part, too, because of the endless struggle to survive. A large number of people lived in the Highlands at this time, perhaps as much as a quarter of the whole Scottish population. They lived in small huts which they shared with animals. An English traveller of the early 1700s was invited into the home of a tacksman, who was one of the wealthier clansmen, and reported his experience (**E**).

E He invited me into his hut which was built like the others, only very long, but without any partition, where the family was at one end and some cattle at the other. He was without shoes, stockings or breeches, in a short coat with a shirt not much longer.

The Highlanders grew a little oats and barley and kept hens, sheep and goats, but they relied chiefly on black cattle. These supplied milk, meat and leather: they were also sold to traders. In summer the cattle were taken up to higher ground to graze. Here people lived in huts like those on Jura (**F**).

Late winter could find Highlanders living in misery. Rain splashed through the turf roofs of their huts, smoke filled the little room in which people and animals crowded together. The store of oatmeal began to run low. Clansmen were sometimes likely to go out raiding to support themselves and their families, stealing cattle especially. As a visitor noted in the 1700s:

G The stealing of cows they call 'lifting', they go out in parties of 10 to 30 men, the principal time for this wicked practice is the Michaelmas moon when the cattle are in a condition fit for markets.

In 1689 Thomas Morer noted down his views of Highland life (**H**). He saw that many were still Catholic (or 'Irish') in belief.

H The Highlanders are not without considerable quantities of corn, yet have not enough to satisfy their numbers and therefore yearly come down with their cattle and trade with Lowlanders for oats and barley. Many not only keep the Irish language but the Irish religion.

Plaids are most in use with 'em, they serve them for clothes by day but were beds in the night at such times as they travelled. These plaids are about 7 or 8 yards long. They cover the whole body with them from the neck to the knees, excepting the right arm. Those who have stockings made 'em of the same piece with their plaids, not knit but sewed together.

Clans, then, were groups of people organised to help one another. The tenants in the little clusters of huts shared their work on the land, struggling to survive in areas where, sometimes, the soil was thin and poor. But clans were, too, groups of people organised for war. It was this that made them such fine soldiers who could so quickly be ready to fight. After Culloden the Government smashed their fighting strength and cut away the power of the chiefs.

F *Shieling huts*

BURGH LIFE

The view in **A** shows the burgh of Perth. It was one of the most important places in Scotland at this time. There are two clues in the drawing that show why Perth had grown to a size of over 5000 people. The river allowed trading boats to sail there, and the great Church of St John was clearly very important. Kings and wealthy landowners encouraged the growth of burghs (for they made Scotland a wealthier place) and gave privileges to them, allowing them to control the trade inside the burgh and in the nearby area. Until around 1670 only royal burghs were supposed to trade with countries overseas. This overseas trade helped places like Aberdeen and Dundee to grow. An English visitor in 1598 listed the sorts of things that Scottish merchants carried in their ships (**B**).

A Perth in the late 1600s

B **The people of Western Scotland carry into Ireland herrings, coal, whisky and bring out yarn and cow hides or silver. The Eastern Scots carry into France coarse cloth – both linen and woollen which be narrow and shrink in the wetting. They also carry wool, skins of goats, fish taken in the Scottish sea and after smoked or otherwise dried and salted and they bring from there salt and wines. But the chief traffic of the Scots is at Campshire (with the Dutch) where they carry salt, skins and bring corn, at Bordeaux where they carry clothes and skins and bring wines, prunes, walnuts and chestnuts, thirdly within the Baltic Sea whither they carry clothes and skins and bring flax, hemp, iron, pitch and tar. And lastly in England whither they carry linen clothes, yarn, salt and bring wheat, oats, beans and like things.**

C Merchants with a pack of goods

C shows a discussion between two merchants who are standing by newly arrived packs of goods. Notice that the pack has a mark on it showing to whom it belonged: remember that many people could not read at this time.

Burghs also traded with people from nearby areas, for all sorts of craftsmen lived and worked there, making goods for sale.

D and **E** show just two of the many crafts that flourished in burghs: these men are making clothes and shoes. The shoemaker (or 'cordiner') is also making a sale to a lady customer. Craftsman like these (**F**) worked by hand, so it took a great deal of time and skill to create something. Customers who bought from them expected their purchases to last!

F *Craftsmen commonly found in burghs*

smiths	hat and bonnet makers	
bakers (or 'baxters')	wrights	glovers
tailors	coopers	goldsmiths
candlemakers	furriers	skinners
brewers	masons	saddlers
weavers (or 'websters')		
shoemakers (or 'cordiners')		

The craftsmen organised themselves into groups of trades working at the same sorts of crafts, called 'guilds'. This meant that the craftsmen could control who joined their guild. A man wishing to join had to serve seven years as an apprentice, learning from a master craftsman, and had to produce an example of his work to prove his skill, as the rule of 1570 (**G**) from the Dunfermline Hammermen's Guild demonstrates.

G **Each craft apprentice, before being admitted to the Guild, must make an example of his work, the same to be passed as satisfactory, by three expert craftsmen of the Guild.**

D A tailor

Cordiners (shoemakers)

J *West Port, St Andrews*

Each guild had a leader (or 'deacon') who checked that apprentices were properly trained, and examined goods for sale to make sure they were suitable and at the price that had been decided by the burgh. Sometimes this led to quarrels and to punishments for guild members, as in this example from Glasgow:

H **Alexander Scott, baxter, is found in the wrong for stopping George Young, deacon, from entering his booth to exercise the rule about weighing of his bread. Also William Neilson is found in the wrong for injuring of George his deacon and for baking and having poor-quality bread.**

I *Aberdeen's market cross*

Craftsmen like those in **E** had places from which to sell their goods, but many folk came to burghs to buy and sell at open-air stalls. All burghs, therefore, had large areas where markets were held, usually around a market cross (**I**). The members of the burgh (the burgesses) made sure that they controlled this too. Selling could only begin after the market bell had been rung, and burgesses had to be served before other people. Goods for sale had to be weighed at a public weighing machine (called a 'tron'). The people who wanted to sell goods had to pay tolls to the burgh for the privilege of doing this.

These rules show how carefully the burgesses controlled their burgh, using the privileges that they had been given in a charter. The burgesses chose their town council which made the rules that had to be obeyed in the burgh. Royal burghs even chose their own members of parliament. Only a man with money could become a burgess, for a fee had to be paid for the privilege, a fee that only reasonably successful merchants and members of craft guilds could afford. A man who married the daughter of a burgess could join the privileged group who were burgesses, and sons were often able to follow their fathers, paying smaller fees than those charged to outsiders. **J** shows the entry to the burgh of St Andrews – it is a clear sign that the burgesses meant to control all who came in and out of the place.

But the people who crowded together in burghs could easily pass diseases to one another. It was not easy to keep such places clean in the days before drains and sewers: all the filth (including sewage) produced by a household was often simply tipped out onto the streets. From time to time in this period Scotland was troubled by the plague spread by the fleas carried by black rats. In 1513 King James IV sent out orders to be declared from burgh market crosses (**K**).

Burgh life had its risks as well as its advantages.

K

- If any household has an infected person they must nail upon their stairs and doors a piece of white cloth.
- No person is to leave their house, if there is anyone in it with the plague, under pain of death.
- All infected persons who find themselves cured must remain in their houses for 40 days.
- All animals found wandering the streets to be killed.
- All streets, alleys and gutters to be cleaned.
- No children under the age of 15 to be found on the streets under the pain of putting them in the stocks and beating them with sticks.

Make up a collection of documents that have survived from an old burgh including:
- A list of goods unloaded from a ship
- Rules for dealing with a plague outbreak
- Rules for one of the craft guilds
- Market regulations
- A letter from a man wishing to become a burgess and explaining why he is qualified.

A VISIT TO EDINBURGH

A *Slezer's view of Edinburgh*

Edinburgh is Scotland's capital city and people from all over the world come to visit it. Many visitors came to Edinburgh 300 years ago too. But what would they have seen then? Imagine you are approaching the city from the south. Three hundred years ago you would have seen the view in **A**. What might have impressed you about this sight?

Around 30 000 people lived in the city – a huge number by the standards of Scotland at the time. If you could afford it, you might even have chosen to travel by hackney coach (**B**).

C *Paul Sandby's drawing of Edinburgh High Street*

B *Rules for hackney coaches, 1672*

- All hackney coaches to be numbered.

- Coach hire from Edinburgh to Leith to be twelve shillings for three persons.

- Coaches must neither trot nor gallop on the streets of the town.

- Masters and owners of coaches are responsible for their servants' misbehaviour.

- Only burgesses and persons obtaining the Council's order may keep hackney coaches.

As you journey up the High Street you might well see local people like those in **C** which was drawn by a young English artist in the 1700s. However, we don't have to imagine what a visit was like: Thomas Morer came to Edinburgh in 1689 and has left us an account of his visit (**D**).

D Edinburgh consists chiefly of one fair street from west to east about a mile long, from the Castle to Holyrood. Their old houses are cased with boards and have oval windows without glass. Their new houses are made of stone with good windows and glazed and so lofty that 5 or 6 storeys is an ordinary height and one row of buildings there is with no less than fourteen.

Most of the houses, as they are separated into several tenements, have as many landlords as storeys. Their stairs built out of the street are sometime so steep, narrow and fenceless that it requires care to go up and down for fear of falling. But in their new houses it is better, the staircase being made within the building.

On the south side was a lake but this is now drained and a narrow street built upon it which they call Cowgate, between which and the High Street there are many little lanes. The pride of Edinburgh is the Parliament Yard, square and well paved. Its western boundary is the Parliament House. In the first floor level with the yard are three or four booksellers and as many goldsmiths. On the north of the city is the physick garden with 2700 sorts of plants. The manager of it has a small salary allowed by the apothecaries of the town.

Edinburgh contained many churches, Holyrood Palace, the Castle and a University. No doubt you might have seen many students in the streets as you travelled, not all of them working, as this extract from Edinburgh records makes clear:

E The town council of Edinburgh orders the tailor who lives in Bell's Wynd to remove the billiard board from this house because too many students go there to play billiards and ignore their studies.

As a traveller back in time you would certainly also notice the smell. The people who lived in the tall buildings were in the habit of flinging waste (including sewage) out of their windows to the cry of 'Gardy loo'. The council never seemed to be able to solve this problem in spite of passing laws.

In 1701 a visitor, Joseph Taylor, grumbled about the state of the city:

F Every street shows the nastiness of the inhabitants, the excrements lie in heaps. In a morning the scent was so offensive that we were forced to hold our noses and take care where we trod for fear of disobliging our shoes and to walk in the middle of the street – for fear of an accident on our heads. The lodgings are as nasty as the streets and washed so seldom that the dirt is enough to be pared off with a shovel. We have the best lodgings and yet our room looked into a place they call the close, full of nastiness. 'Tis a common thing for a man or woman to go into these closes at all times of the day to ease nature.

It would have been a relief to escape from the streets and today it is still possible to visit a house that you could also have visited 300 years ago. It is called 'Gladstone's Land' (**G**) – a 'land' was the name for a tall building.

In the early 1600s, Thomas Gledstanes, a merchant, had this house built. It is in the Lawnmarket which was the place where goods made in the countryside – especially woollen and linen cloth – were sold. Each floor of the house was rented to a tenant, with Thomas himself living on the third floor. Visitors to

Edinburgh from other countries were often surprised by the way different classes of people might share a house like this: the Gledstanes' first-floor tenant was a gentleman, Sir James Creichton. This room (**H**) has been furnished by the National Trust for Scotland to show what a room of the time might have looked like.

The ceiling has been painted in a fashion popular in the 1600s. You can see why Thomas Gledstanes was probably quite proud of his house.

If you were to stay on until night-time, the darkness would have seemed quite alarming, for Edinburgh at this time did not have proper street lighting. Perhaps it's wisest to return to modern times.

G Gladstone's Land

H The Painted Room

1 Do you know what a 'probate inventory' is? It's a list of someone's property that is written down when that person dies. Look at H and make up a probate inventory for this room.

2 What if there were a plan to totally alter Gladstone's Land, turning it into a modern shop? Would it matter if this part of our heritage vanished? Design a poster to attract people to a meeting about this. Make clear your point of view.

3 Make up the sort of diary entry for 300 years ago that a visitor to Edinburgh might have written. Make clear who you are — an ordinary visitor from the Scottish countryside and a rich visitor from London might have very different views.

Daily Life

RICH AND POOR

A *Craigievar Castle*

B *Meals in Ochtertyre House*

Sunday 25 September 1737

Dinner   Skink and tripe
Beefe rost pieces
Hams boyld
Tongues and lure
Hard fish and plumb pudding
Calves head hasht and peas
Partridges with cellery
Turkeyes rost and larded
Geess rost
Pidgeons rost
Tarts and collard pige
Beefe for servants pieces

Supper   Veal rost joints
Pidgeons in a pye
Spinage and eggs and artichoaks
Puddings smoakt beefe and pickles
Foulls for broath

Monday 16 January 1738

Dinner   Green keall
Foull rost
Beefe for servants pieces

Supper   Collops
Mutton rost joints
Eggs and sallad magundey
Foulls for broath
Ducks in a pye

Saturday 29 January 1739

Dinner   Cockie leeking foulls in it
Pork boyld pieces
Hare collops and a pease pudding
Turkeyes rost
Mutton rost joints
Partridges stewd
Tarts and ane omlite
Mutton for servants and broath joints

Supper   Fish broyld
Cold turkey tarts hogs cheek and eggs
Smoak beefe and butter

Most of the buildings that we can still see today which were constructed between 1500 and 1750 were put up by rich people. If we study them carefully we can see how life changed, for the earlier buildings often look as if they were constructed to be strong enough to keep out attackers. By the end of the period, wealthy people were having homes built like the House of Dun (see page 3). Look at **A**. This is Craigievar Castle, in the Aberdeenshire countryside.

Does it look as if Craigievar was built with the main aim of keeping out attackers? Notice all the windows. This home was built in the years 1610–26 for William Forbes. He was a very successful Aberdeen merchant who traded with Baltic countries. The castle suggests that a rich person still needed to feel safe: it does not look able to resist a strong attack, however. In fact this was a splendid and comfortable home and shows how those who had enough money were changing their lives. In the last 100 years of our period, especially, they filled their homes with elegant and comfortable furniture, fine linen and tapestries. They ate well, too. Look at **B**. These are the menus of main meals eaten on just three days in the home of a wealthy person.

Wealthy families liked to have paintings made of themselves. **C** was painted in 1740 by Jeremiah Davison. It shows James Douglas and his family. James Douglas was the Earl of Morton. He was not only rich, he was also well educated, and very interested in the science and culture of the time.

The life lived by this Earl of Morton was very different from the one lived by his ancestors in the 1500s. They were often in conflict with others and used their armed tenants to back their quarrels: this Earl lived at peace, travelled throughout Britain and Europe and sought wealth, comfort and elegance, not military power.

Few Scots people lived so comfortable a life. Far more were likely to live in misery; for the poorest people in Scotland at this time, life was very bleak indeed. All sorts of reasons might plunge people into a life where they were in real danger of starving to death. They might be ill or crippled, they might suffer an accident or be too old to work. There were also times when some people simply couldn't find work. There were other times when the crops failed and people starved. In the 1690s, especially, crop failures led to a terrible famine that resulted in sights like those described in 1699 by Robert Sibbald (**D**):

C *James Douglas and his family*

D For want some die in the wayside, some drop down in the streets, the poor sucking babes are starving for want of milk. Everyone may see Death in the face of the poor that abound everywhere, the thinness of the visage [face], their ghostly looks, their feebleness. And it is not only common wandering beggars that are in this case, but many householders who lived well by their labour are now by want forced to abandon their dwellings. They and their little ones must beg.

How were the poor cared for? The next sources provide clues. **E** is a law of 1556 passed by Dundee Burgh.

E It is statute [law] that no beggars be found in this town but they were born here and that are too feeble, weak, or old to work for their living. If they are not old and of the burgh and still beg, they will be burned on the cheek and banished [from] this burgh.

F dates from 1616 and is a law passed in Aberdeen.

F The magistrates and kirk session ordered that no beggars get any alms within this burgh except such as bear the town's token. The town must be cleared of beggars from other places so that the town's own poor may be better helped.

Many burghs gave tokens like **G** to those local people who were given permission to beg.

G Beggars' tokens

In 1672 an Act was passed by Parliament:

H Good laws have been frustrated because there has been no place where poor people might be set to work, nor persons appointed to be in charge of them: His Majesty orders that burghs provide correction houses for beggars, vagabonds and idle persons and appoint masters who may set these poor persons to work.

For people unable to work by reason of age, infirmity or disease, the heritors [landowners] are to bear the burden of keeping the poor, deciding places for them to live in that they may be supplied by contributions at the parish kirk.

Poor persons able to work be offered to the people of each parish to become apprentices or servants. And His Majesty empowers the masters of the correction houses, in case of the disobedience of poor people, to use all manner of severity and correction by whipping. It shall be lawful for coalmasters, saltmasters and others who have manufactories to seize any vagabonds or beggars and put them to work.

I An Aberdeen street name

Some former houses of correction are marked today by street names (**I**).

Although the Government allowed local areas to raise taxes to pay for the poor, most were not willing to do this. Instead the poor had to depend on the money provided by the ministers and the kirk session: this money came from special collections for the poor, from fines and charges and from money sometimes left for the poor by wealthy people when they died. It usually amounted to very little indeed.

1 Look at source B. Could all this food have come from the local area? What is missing that you would expect to find at such a meal today?

2 Source C was painted for Lord Morton. Does that mean that there is any evidence in this picture that can't be trusted? What evidence is there in it of children's toys?

3 Look through the section for information on poor people.
   a List all the ways in which they were helped.
   b Can you think of anything to be said in favour of the law of 1672 (source H)?

EXPLORING INDUSTRIES

Look at **A**. It shows part of the burgh of Culross. The houses have been restored by the National Trust for Scotland, making the burgh a delightful and peaceful place to visit. But a visitor in the early 1600s would have encountered quite different sights. Thick clouds of dark smoke hung over the houses, the banging of makers of iron goods at work rang round the streets, and men blackened with coal dust walked wearily home, for Culross then was an important industrial centre. The people of the burgh prospered and the quality of the houses that we can still see today shows this. They collected seawater in huge shallow iron pans which they then heated over coal fires. The water evaporated, leaving the salt behind. This was a valuable product which people were eager to buy to preserve meat and fish. Ironworkers specialised in making girdles (**B**) for cooking on. Culross girdles were famous throughout Scotland.

A *Culross*

The coal burned by the saltworkers came from a mine that worked for many years – indeed the first miners were medieval monks! In 1575 Sir George Bruce (a descendant of Robert the Bruce) obtained control over the colliery and set about expanding it. He invented a machine called an 'Egyptian wheel' (**C**).

This meant that the water that seeped into the mine (as it extended downwards from its original 10 metres to as much as 75 metres) could be scooped up by an endless chain of buckets.

In 1618 the traveller John Taylor visited Culross and was amazed by this machinery. He wrote about what he saw:

B *A girdle*

C *Sir George Bruce's 'Egyptian wheel'*

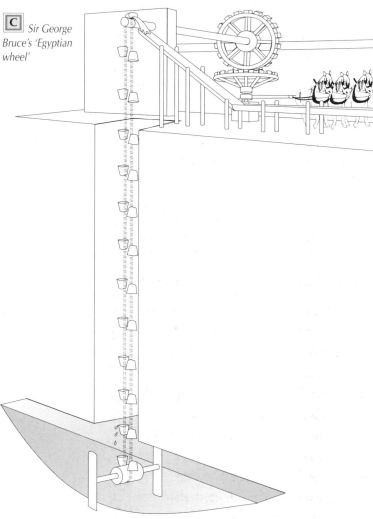

D **The sea at certain places doth leak into the mine which is all conveyed to one well where he hath a device like a horse-mill that, with 3 horses and a great chain of iron going downwards with 36 buckets fastened to the chain; of which 18 go down to be filled and 18 ascend up to be emptied, which do empty themselves into a trough that conveys the water into the sea again.**

Taylor saw 50 hugh saltpans being worked, producing around a hundred tons of salt every week that was then sent around Scotland, to England and even shipped to Germany. But what especially amazed visitors was that Sir George's mine workings ran under the sea. Even James VI came to view this amazing sight. John Taylor wrote:

E **The mine hath two ways into it, the one by sea and the other by land. Now men may object, how can a man go into a mine the entrance of it being into the sea? To which I answer, at low water, the sea being ebbed away and a great part of the sand bare, upon this sand (being mixed with rocks and craggs) did the master of this**

great work build a round circular frame of stone so high that the sea can neither dissolve the stones nor yet overflow the height. Within this frame workmen did dig down. At last they found coal and did dig forward so that in eight and twenty years they have dug more than a mile under the sea that where men are at work below, a hundred of the greatest ships in Britain may sail over their heads.

Sights like those to be seen at Culross were very rare indeed in Scotland; a centre of production was much more likely to look like the one in picture **F**. This is Preston Mill, near Dunbar. Like much of Culross, it too is owned by the National Trust for Scotland, and parts of the building date from the 1600s. Notice the wheel: it is turned by a flow of water pushing it round, and drives milling machinery for grinding corn. The unusually-shaped roof covers the kiln where corn was dried before being milled: the damp heat escaped from a hole in this roof. Water power was often used to drive machinery in Scotland and sometimes had to be carried quite a distance before it reached the wheel it turned. **G** shows a wheel that worked machinery in a lead mine in Dumfriesshire. The drawing was made in the mid-1700s by Paul Sandby, an English artist.

F *Preston Mill*

A young Swedish visitor called Henry Kalmeter came to Scotland in 1719 and was especially interested in industries like **G**. He kept a record of his travels – **H** comes from this journal:

H On May 26 I came to Leadhills, the country round about is very mountainous and the weather is so appalling that the snow often covers the huts, where people live. The workmen, who do not exceed 100 in number, have free housing but must rest content with five or sixpence a day and carry the ore to the foot of the shaft. When the ore comes to the surface they take the best of it, which by hammering can be made pure, and lay it out in heaps. There are three smelting houses.

G *Sandby's drawing of a lead mine*

People who worked in salt and coal mines suffered from harsh changes in the law in the 1600s, beginning with a law of 1606 which stated that no-one could employ a collier or saltworker without a statement releasing the worker from his previous job. These laws turned the workers into serfs who took jobs in collieries and saltpans for life and were regarded as their masters' property. Women and children worked in mines too, carrying coal back to the surface. The churchmen, landowners and merchants of the time did not protest at these fierce laws passed by the Scottish Parliament, laws that were not finally abolished until the late 1700s. In 1641 Parliament even insisted:

I Coal hewers and salterers work all the six days of the week: everyone who is idle shall pay 20 shillings for every day.

Some other employers tried to apply similar conditions but it was in the coal mines that they worked most effectively: for the coal workers of early modern Scotland, life became worse, not better.

1 Use sources **A** to **E** to write an account like the one Sir George Bruce might have given to a visitor he was showing round Culross.

2 Can you think of any reasons why harsh laws about colliers and saltworkers were so easily passed and didn't cause protests?

3 Examine **F** and **G** and explain two different ways in which water power was used to turn wheels.

WOMEN'S LIVES

In 1636 Sir William Brereton visited Edinburgh. As an Englishman he noticed the differences in people's clothing compared with those he was used to seeing as he walked about the streets. He wrote:

A **Many women wear plaids which are cast over their heads and cover their faces on both sides and would reach almost to the ground but that they pluck them up and wear them cast under their arms. Some ancient women wear satin straight-bodied gowns and short little cloaks. Young maids, not married, are all bareheaded.**

In 1679 Thomas Kirke added further detail to this glimpse of what the women of this time looked like (**B**).

B **The meaner go barefoot and barehead with two black elf locks on either side of their faces. Some of them have scarce any clothes at all save part of their bedclothes pinned about their shoulders.**

---

1 The women seen by these English visitors lived in ways that were often very different from today. Explore all the material in this section to find as many changes as possible between life for women then and now. Write them down as a list.

2 Has everything that has happened since been a change for the better? Give reasons for your answer.

Most of the paintings of this period that show the women of the time are of the wealthy. **C** is unusual, therefore, because it shows an ordinary person in the early 1700s. This woman worked as a 'henwife' for a rich family. She looked after the hens and collected their eggs. Ordinary women faced endless hours of work. They had to cook, bake, wash, spin thread for clothing, mend clothing and generally keep their families going, though they had very little to manage

C *The Henwife*

on. They also had to work outside the home, for families needed every little amount of money that could be earned. For most women this meant helping with farmwork. **D** shows some of their duties.

D **Rule of 1656 made for the wives of farm workers by Midlothian magistrates. Women were expected to help cut corn, gather hay, cut peats, cart and spread manure, take corn for threshing, help with winnowing, clean byres and take food to animals.**

Some women worked at lime kilns, others were employed down coal mines to carry coal in baskets up to the surface. Many women found jobs as servants. They were especially used as washerwomen and laundrymaids. Sir William Brereton did not think much of the way that they washed bedclothes (**E**).

E **Their linen is sluttishly washed by women's feet: after their linen is put into a great broad low tub of water then (their clothes being tucked up above their knees) they step into the tub and tread it and trample it with their feet until it be sufficiently cleansed: bedding doth so strongly taste and smell of lint and other noisesome savours as that when I came to bed I was constrained to hold my nose.**

During his travels in the late 1600s, John Slezer came upon such washerwomen and added them to his sketch of Dundee (**F**).

Another artist sketched women at work during his travels in the Highlands (**G**). The two women on the left are turning corn into flour by grinding it between two stones. The upper stone of this 'quern' is turned, rubbing the seeds into a powder. The other women

F *Slezer's sketch of washerwomen*

G *Highland women*

are thickening cloth by soaking, trampling and shrinking it in a process called 'waulking'. Notice that the only man in the picture is not working!

Women who had recently given birth to children but had lost some (or all) of them sometimes found work as 'wet nurses'. They fed the babies of wealthy women who chose not to provide the milk themselves. The medical books of the time gave advice as to the sort of women who would make a suitable wet nurse. One of them suggested:

H **As the nurse is, so will the child be, by means of the nourishment which it draweth from her and in sucking her it will draw in both the vices of her body and mind. She ought to have a sweet voice to please the child and likewise she ought to have a clear pronunciation that he may not learn an ill accent from her, as usually red-haired nurses have.**

At least women of the 1600s were generally freer to choose whom to marry than women of earlier times. Parents continued to be very important in influencing whom a girl might marry, but the days of parents meeting to settle a marriage without consulting the couple involved, were fading away. A bride's parents were expected to provide her with a 'tocher' (a dowry) that might consist of land, clothes, money, even furniture. The daughter of a wealthy and generous father, therefore, might find that there were a number of men who were eager to marry her. When the Marquis of Tweedale married the daughter of the very powerful Duke of Lauderdale, one wedding guest at least felt he'd married for wealth and position, for he said of the girl:

I **She is very homely and like a monkey clothed with gold and silver.**

Future brides were generally expected to be quiet and modest. Certainly the better off were not expected to take the initiative. The Earl of Morton observed:

J **It is a great disgrace for a gentlewoman to woo and then be disappointed.**

When a woman married, she handed over her life to her husband. During the service she promised:

K **To study to please and obey her husband, serving him in all things that be godly and honest, she is in subjection and under governance of her husband.**

The husband decided what was to happen to the wife's property and where she was to live: she couldn't even begin a legal case without his agreement. It was possible to obtain a divorce for adultery and (after 1573) for desertion, but it was a very long and difficult process. The Church regarded marriage as far too important to allow easy divorce. Once married, women faced the health hazards of frequent childbirth, for they were expected to have many children since the risk was so high of children dying young.

Married women with wealth still had to work, overseeing the servants and even managing affairs when husbands were away. In their leisure they spent time sewing, playing musical instruments like the lute and the harpsichord and reading the increasing number of books that were available from the late 1500s onwards. For most ordinary women, however, there was little leisure time: work, caring for the family and the endless struggle to survive occupied their lives.

CRIMES AND PUNISHMENTS

Scotland in the 1500s and 1600s did not have a proper police force. Yet men often owned daggers and swords and many had pistols. So quarrels that became violent could easily lead to killings. In 1598 the Edinburgh Town Council tried to find an answer (**A**).

> **A** **In the past there have been several stabbings and murders committed in the town with no-one trying to stop them. Because of this it is ordered that every merchant and craftsman have in their stalls and shops as many axes as they have servants and to come speedily to the aid of the provost and the baillies when trouble breaks out.**

Crimes at this time included the same sorts of offences still common today, crimes like stealing and cheating, violent attacks and murder. But there were also crimes that no longer exist and which resulted from the religious beliefs of the time. The Kirk tried to insist that behaviour it did not approve of was punished so that, for example, giving birth to a child when the parents were not married was regarded as a most serious crime. So seriously did some women fear punishment that there were cases of mothers killing their babies lest their offence be discovered. Strong religious beliefs sometimes allowed one group in power to fiercely punish those who differed with them. In 1685, for example, two women were found guilty of supporting and helping the Covenanters. The result was that Margaret McLaughlan, who was in her sixties, and the 18-year-old Margaret Wilson, were tied to a stake below the flood level of the mouth of the River Bladenoch near Wigtown. As the tide came in, the water rose and the women drowned.

Most serious of all was the belief in witchcraft. Medieval Scots had widely assumed that, just as saints could intervene in their lives to help them, so might all sorts of spirits and fairies. The Reformation, however, changed views on how such beliefs should be treated. Scots who visited the Continent were influenced by beliefs there, such as those of the leading Protestant John Calvin, who wrote:

> **B** **The Bible teaches us that there are witches and that they must be slain. God commands that all witches and enchantresses shall be put to death.**

King James VI was so concerned about witchcraft that he wrote a book about it. In it he described the behaviour of witches (**C**).

> **C** **Some in the likeness of a little beast or fowl will come and pierce through whatsoever house or church though all the passages are closed, by whatsoever opening the air may enter in at.**

D shows James questioning four witches.

D

Between 1560 and the final ending of the laws against witchcraft in 1736, it is probable that as many as 4000 people in Scotland were executed for being witches (women) or warlocks (men). Some of them seem to have believed that they actually did have special powers, but many were picked out for other reasons. Women living alone were especially vulnerable. People looked for someone to blame for misfortunes such as sudden death, a diseased animal or a crop failure. Most of those who died were women and generally they came from among the ranks of ordinary people.

During a period when divisions and conflicts were all too common, some people were regarded as criminals because they supported a different side. In 1645 James, Lord Ogilvy, awaited execution for supporting the royalists at a time when those opposed to the Stewart family were in power. Just before the sentence was carried out, his sister, mother and wife were allowed to visit James as he lay in a cell in St Andrews Castle. Guards took no notice as the visitors left, holding handkerchiefs to their weeping eyes. But in fact one of them was James himself! He had managed to exchange clothes with his sister. She spent the night under the bedclothes whilst her brother escaped. Next day guards discovered what had happened. They kept her locked up for two days before releasing her.

People accused of crimes could, until 1708, be tortured. Those accused of witchcraft suffered especially, as their accusers tried to make them confess and give the names of the other witches in their group (or 'coven'). The agony that they suffered led many who were innocent to declare that they were guilty and to give the names of other innocent people. **E** is the story of just one 'witch'. It was written in 1591.

E **Within the town of Tranent there dwelleth David Seaton who had a maid called Geillis Duncan who used to secretly leave her master's house and help all who were troubled with any kind of sickness and did perform many matters most miraculous. David Seaton began to grow very inquisitive and examined her. Her master, to find out the truth, did, with the help of others, torment her with the torture of pilliwinks [thumbscrews] upon her fingers and wrenching her head with a rope which is a most cruel torment. Yet, would she not confess anything, whereupon they, suspecting that she had been marked by the devil, made search of her and found the mark in the forepart of her throat; which being found, she confessed that all her doings were done by enticements of the devil. She confessed that she took a black toad and did hang it by the heels for three days and collected the venom as it dropped.**

Those searching for the devil's mark did so by jabbing a long needle into the witch's body, for it was believed that at the point where the devil had bitten his servant, no pain would be felt. Those strong enough to avoid confessing might still be killed in the belief that they were so much in the devil's power that this gave them extra strength. Some were tortured by having the bones in their legs broken.

Witches were killed by being burned alive. Others condemned to death might be beheaded with an axe, hanged, or (in Aberdeen and Edinburgh) beheaded by a machine called a 'maiden' (**F**). The crimes for which people might be executed did not just include murder: in 1556, for example, Henry Wynd died because he was guilty of forgery.

These ferocious punishments were aimed at frightening wrongdoers. Indeed bodies might be left hanging and heads left on spikes on town walls for many days as a warning to others. Few people were

punished by imprisonment, for, though burghs were supposed to build tollbooths with cells in them, the costs of a prison involved gaoler's wages too. Fines and various sorts of public humiliation were more popular. People might be fastened to the beam of the tron by an iron collar or locked into the stocks for several hours. **G** shows an example of one of these collars (or 'jougs') as well as thumbscrews, handcuffs and manacles.

F *A maiden*

In 1692 a Speyside man was condemned:

H **To be nailed by the lug [ear] with an iron nail to the post and to stand there for the space of one hour.**

G *Thumbscrews, handcuffs and a joug*

This form of punishment only ended when either the victim pulled away or someone cut off part of the ear. Quarrelsome women and women who spread wicked stories about others might have an iron helmet fitted with a piece that clamped over the tongue, fastened on them. This was called 'the branks'. Catching criminals was made easier by the problems of travel at the time and by the fact that most people lived in little townships where everyone knew everyone else.

1 Use the material in this section to write an account of catching, questioning and punishing a witch:
  a as it might have been written by the accused, determined to leave a record of the truth
  b as it might have been written by one of her accusers.
2 'People then must have been much more cruel.' Do you think this is a satisfactory explanation for the treatment of people accused of crimes in the 1500s and 1600s?

LOOKING BACK

The period covered in this book is crammed with all sorts of events. The activities suggested here ask you to think about the whole period.

1 Time

Time-lines are useful ways of showing what has happened. But the past is crowded with events. What we choose to pick out and put on a time-line will depend on what we think is important.

a Make up a time-line for the whole of this period from the point of view of a very devout member of the Kirk living in 1750.

b Make up a time-line for the whole of this period from the point of view of a very enthusiastic supporter of the Stewart royal family, living in 1750.

c Make up your own time-line, choosing just 10 or 12 events.

How do these time-lines differ?

2 Change

Look back over all that happened in the period 1500 to 1750.

a What do you think is the single most important change to have happened in this period?

b Suggest a change that made life better.

c Suggest a change that made life worse.

3 Cause and consequence

The period opens with the Battle of Flodden fought between Scots and English soldiers. It closes with England and Scotland united as part of the United Kingdom. Think back over all that happened and work out as many causes as possible that explain the creation of a United Kingdom.

4 Evidence

During your work on this book you have studied several different sorts of historical evidence.

a Make up a list of all the different sorts of evidence you have used (for example, you have used drawings made at the time, you have used paintings made since the time).

b Are some of these sources more valuable than others? If you could choose only one, which would it be?

5 People's past lives

The people who lived in the period 1500–1750 were just as intelligent as we are, yet sometimes their lives seem very different.

a What aspect of past life from these times have you found to be most strange and peculiar?

b If, by saying, 'I wish I had been there', you could go back to a particular place and event from this period, what would you choose? Why?

6 Heritage

a Do you think we ought all to pay money to the Government (as taxes) so that entry to museums and old buildings can be very cheap, or free?

b Does 'heritage' just mean old buildings and objects? What else might it include?

The Stewart family dynasty in early modern times

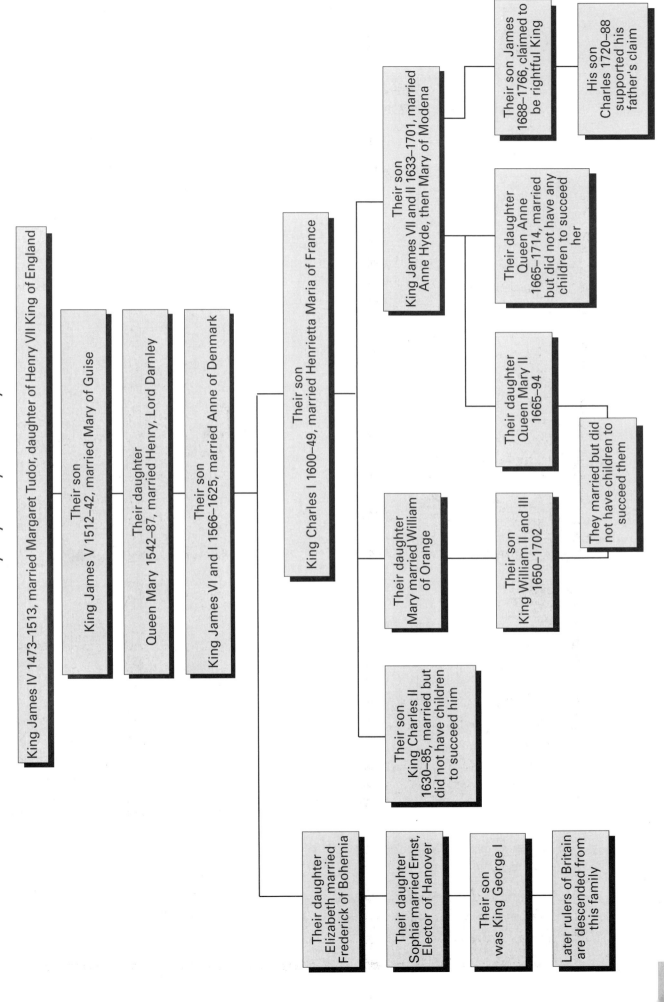

King James IV 1473–1513, married Margaret Tudor, daughter of Henry VII King of England

Their son
King James V 1512–42, married Mary of Guise

Their daughter
Queen Mary 1542–87, married Henry, Lord Darnley

Their son
King James VI and I 1566–1625, married Anne of Denmark

Their son
King Charles I 1600–49, married Henrietta Maria of France

Their son
King Charles II 1630–85, married but did not have children to succeed him

Their daughter
Elizabeth married Frederick of Bohemia

Their daughter
Sophia married Ernst, Elector of Hanover

Their son
was King George I

Later rulers of Britain are descended from this family

Their daughter
Mary married William of Orange

Their son
King William II and III 1650–1702

They married but did not have children to succeed them

Their daughter
Queen Mary II 1665–94

Their son
King James VII and II 1633–1701, married Anne Hyde, then Mary of Modena

Their daughter
Queen Anne 1665–1714, married but did not have any children to succeed her

Their son James 1688–1766, claimed to be rightful King

His son Charles 1720–88 supported his father's claim

SCOTTISH LIFE 1500–1750 TIME-LINE

Date	Event	Reign
1503	James IV marries Margaret Tudor	
1507	First printing press in Scotland	
1513	Battle of Flodden: death of James	James IV 1488–1513
1513–28	Minority of James V	
1528	Patrick Hamilton burned for heresy	
1542	Battle of Solway Moss: Death of James V	James V 1513–42
1546	George Wishart burned for heresy	
1547	Battle of Pinkie	
1560	John Knox writes his *Book of Discipline*	Mary 1542–67
1561–67	Period of Mary's rule in Scotland	
1565	Marriage of Mary and Lord Darnley	
1566	Murder of Riccio	
1567	Murder of Darnley. Marriage of Mary and Bothwell. Mary forced to abdicate	
1583	Founding of Edinburgh University	
1587	Execution of Mary	James VI 1567–1625
1592	'Golden Acts' establishing the Presbyterian Church systems	
1603	James VI succeeds Elizabeth I as ruler of England. James monarch of both countries	
1605	Beginning of the plantation of Ulster	
1610	Restoration of bishops	
1638	The National Covenant	
1639	The Bishops War begins	Charles I 1625–49
1649	Charles I executed	
1650	Battle of Dunbar	
1651	Charles II crowned at Scone	
1651	Battle of Worcester	Commonwealth 1651–60
1660	Restoration of Charles II	
1666	The Pentland uprising	
1670	Death penalty for preaching at conventicles	Charles II 1660–85
1681–87	'The Killing Time'	
1688	'Glorious Revolution' – England deposes James VII	James VII 1685–88
1689	Battle of Killiecrankie	
1692	Massacre of Glencoe	
1695	Founding of the Bank of Scotland	William and Mary 1689–1702
1698	First expedition to Darien	
1707	Union of Scottish and English Parliaments	Anne 1702–14
1715	Jacobite uprising: Battle of Sheriffmuir	
1719	Jacobite uprising	
1725	Malt Tax riots	George I 1714–27
1727	Royal Bank of Scotland established	
1745	Jacobite uprising led by Prince Charles	
1746	Battle of Culloden	
1747	Abolition of heritable jurisdictions	George II 1727–60
1754	Founding of Golfing Society of St Andrews – later Royal and Ancient	